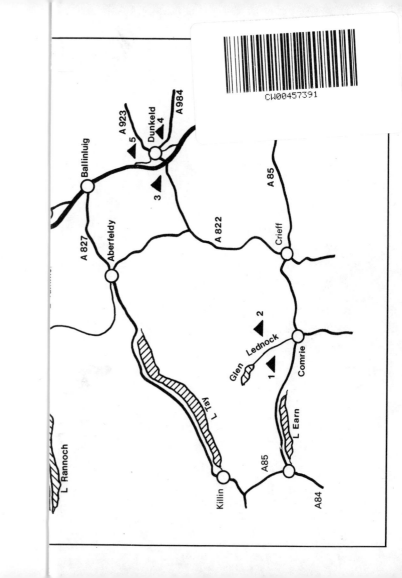

Creag Dubh and Craig-a-Barns

Dave Cuthbertson

SCOTTISH MOUNTAINEERING CLUB

CREAG DUBH AND CRAIG-A-BARNS

First published in Britain 1983 by
The Scottish Mountaineering Club, Edinburgh

ISBN 0 907521 08 8

Filmset by Advanced Filmsetters (Glasgow) Ltd
Printed in Great Britain by Bell and Bain Ltd., Glasgow
Bound by Hunter & Foulis Ltd., Edinburgh

Contents

Illustrations

Illustrations, continued

Acknowledgements

For help with gradings, route descriptions, and for general criticism, I express warm thanks to the following: Rab Anderson, Pete Billesburgh, Ian Duckworth, Murray Hamilton, Gerry Handren, Derek Jamieson, Duncan McCallum, Spider MacKenzie, Neil Morrison, Kenny Spence, Roy Williamson. Special thanks for unstinted photographic work go to Calum Fraser and Gary Latter; also to C. Lyn Jones and Peter Hodgkiss for editing and production.

Scottish Mountaineering Club

The Scottish Mountaineering Club deplore the use of obscene words and phrases for route names but as many route names in this Guide have already appeared in print and are in common use they have been retained.

The S.M.C. will not in future accept route names of an obscene or suggestive nature.

Introduction

Taking into consideration the unreliable weather experienced in the British Isles over the last few years, it is understandable that climbers would focus interest on lower lying areas rather than on mountain crags. With so much new route activity on newly discovered crags, coupled with renewed interest in free climbing, the need for a new guide is clearly established.

This is the first S.M.C. publication to cover climbing on some of Scotland's finest road-side crags. These lie on, or are close by, the A9 between Perth and Newtonmore. Here, enthusiasts can enjoy the sport, not only during the summer season, but throughout the whole year.

Four previously unrecorded areas have been introduced: Craig Varr, Farm Crag, Birnam Quarry and Glen Lednock.

Strictly speaking, Glen Lednock is outside the area, but its proximity to the A9 and its selection of good quality climbs certainly justify its inclusion.

Access

The inclusion of a crag and of route descriptions in this guidebook does not imply right of access or the right to climb. All the crags described lie on privately owned land and future access depends to a large extent on the behaviour of those climbing now. We should all adopt the highest standards with regard to removal of litter and with avoidance of disturbance to stock or of damage to walls. No one should camp or light fires without asking permission of the landowner.

Notes on the Use of the Guide

Grades

The currently accepted system has been used as follows: moderate, difficult, very difficult, severe, hard severe, mild very severe, very severe and hard very severe. For climbs in the extreme category, the open ended E system is used. This is a sub-division of the extreme grade ranging from E1 to E6—the top grade at present. The E grade is an overall assessment of a climb's difficulty and is used in conjunction with a numerical technical grade to give some idea of the hardest move on each individual pitch. The technical grades in this guide range from 4a–6b (7a being the highest grade to date) and are used only on mild very severe climbs and above. A further subdivision of " + " and " − " is also used.

Aid

Aid elimination plays a significant part in the development of modern, hard, free climbing and is encouraged.

Cleaning is standard practice on a new route, whereas top-roping is not. It is hoped that the latter will not be performed.

With so many excellent protection devices available, pegs are seldom necessary. Most of the climbs in this guide are adequately protected without their use. Climbers should take note and reject the use of pegs on climbs which have previously been climbed without. Inevitably, illicit pegs find their way on to some routes and should, if possible, be removed. Fixed protection should be left *in situ* as continual placement and removal causes considerable damage to the rock. Any pegs needed for protection or belays will clearly appear in the text.

The following abbreviations are used: P.R.—peg runner; P.A.—peg aid; P.B.—peg belay; N.A.—nut aid; F.A.—first ascent; F.F.A.—first free ascent.

A star system has been used. Three stars indicate that a route is very fine in the author's opinion. However, star quality does not imply that a route without any stars is not worth climbing.

Left and right refer to the climber facing the cliff.

Each section is complete with introduction, access, accommodation and diagrams, etc. Each area is located by a six figure map reference.

New Routes

New routes and amendments should be sent to the New Routes Editor of the S.M.C. Journal. The journal is published annually and contains a Scottish New Routes Section.

General

Climbers are reminded of their responsibility to dispose of litter carefully. Use of rubbish bins rather than boulders is recommended. The ideal solution is to take all debris home.

N.B. *Mountain Rescue*: Dial 999 and ask for Police.

History

The first proper recorded route in this area was Rib Direct on Creag Dubh. However, an article in an early edition of the S.M.J. by Raeburn and Walker shows how climbers had taken an interest in these cliffs as far back as 1903. Indeed, these early writings clearly describe the lines now taken by Fred and the big vegetated gully bounding the left side of Great Wall.

In the late fifties and early sixties development really got under way. On Creag Dubh in 1959, Sullivan and Parkin climbed the obvious line of Nutcracker Chimney. That same year Sullivan returned with Collingham to climb the steeper and more impressive Brute.

About this time the Perth section of the J.M.C.S. and E.U.M.C. added many, now classic, climbs on Polney, including Smith's fine route, The Groove. Campbell went on to explore the overhanging Cave Crags and in a short space of time most of the obvious lines were climbed. Amongst these were Haston's F . . . Face and one of the last great problems—Rat Race. This, Campbell climbed with McLean to produce one of the finest and most sensational aid routes in the Eastern Crags. Campbell continued his exploration of the area and discovered Bonskeid Crag, adding a number of worthwhile routes.

However, it was Creag Dubh which now became the main centre of interest with Haston and the Edinburgh Squirrels leading the development. In October 1964 Haston succeeded in climbing Inbred, the thin crack line on the steepest and smoothest part of Great Wall. The route soon gained a reputation as one of Scotland's most impressive free climbs. In May the following year no less than thirteen new routes were added. This brought the grand total to thirty and completed a period of intense activity prior to publication of the new guide book.

Completion of the guide created little in the way of new route activity and in general the crags lay dormant for a couple of years.

In 1967 the Spence and Porteous partnership emerged from Edinburgh as one of the strongest teams to appear on the Scottish scene since the days of Smith and Marshall.

Spence made his debut with The Hill on Creag Dubh—a bold and serious lead which still commands respect today. To a lesser extent, but in a similar vein, is the little known Way Through on Polney—Dunkeld's hardest free route at that time. During 1971 and 1972 various parties contributed to the cliffs of Creag Dubh. Crockett and Fulton climbed the serious Mighty Piston. Barley and Griffiths added Outspan to the left side of Great Wall. Staff from Glenmore Lodge showed interest with March and Harper contributing LMF, while Fyffe added two, albeit short, routes on the wall left of Oui Oui. These cliffs also witnessed some impressive solo performances, notably Nicolson's ascents of Inbred and King Bee, the former while Shields was engrossed in the second ascent of The Hill. Living in Aviemore, George Shields adopted Creag Dubh as his local crag which resulted in several fine routes. Niagara is probably his best route but he also freed the Minge and Jump So High and soloed Slanting Groove.

In a traditional vein several very impressive aid routes were climbed on Craig-a-Barns, the most impressive being Fall Out, Hang Out and Green Cheese.

1974 brought about the first major development in Glen Lednock, chiefly by naval personnel, Baker and Conway. This partnership climbed a respectable number of good routes including the plum of Glen Lednock—The Great Crack, a line which had already repulsed several strong teams including one led by L. Brown.

On Craig-a-Barns Mick Couston freed the Stank and Gnome Direct, hinting at things to come.

1976–1982: The beginning of a new era in Scotland! Murray Hamilton, one of a group of young Edinburgh climbers, made several significant free ascents of previous aid routes, particularly on Craig-a-Barns. Hamilton with Dave Cuthbertson made a completely free ascent of Rat Catcher—a difficult and serious undertaking. Hamilton's most impressive feat was a virtually free ascent of Rat Race (1 peg on final overhang); at that time Scotland's most outstanding free climb and a major breakthrough in raising standards on rock.

A lull hung over the cliffs of Creag Dubh until the addition of Run Free and Ruff Licks by Dave Cuthbertson. Ed Grindley visited Glen Lednock, freeing the Great Crack and adding his own serious route, The Chancers. On a more recent visit Hamilton completed a fine trilogy with No Place for a Wendy. On Dunkeld's Cave Crag Derek Jameson created the tremendous Warfarin, while visiting American, Mike Graham, made a stylish free ascent of Rat Race. Later on that year Coffin Arete was relieved of its remaining aid sling and re-named High Performance to establish Scotlands first "6a".

Good weather in spring 1979 sparked off a new lease of life in Glen Lednock. Ian Duckworth and Neil Morrison developed Eagle Crag with a whole host of fine little routes. Also at this time Duckworth and

Morrison, this time with Dave Cuthbertson, paid a visit to the glen and in an attempt to free Central Groove a new 6a standard was established with Gabrielle.

After a good start to the summer of 1979 the monsoons persisted, but the die-hards managed to produce Morbidezza on Cave Crag's Upper Tier, an impressive climb up the overhanging prow left of Mousetrap and an important addition to this crag. Towards the end of the year Mal Duff with various clients established the Birnam Quarry with the serious Counting Out Time and Slateford Road.

The first new route of 1980 on Craig-a-Barns took the big wall left of Rat Catcher. Lady Charlotte established herself as the crag's most serious undertaking and became Scotland's first E5. Hot on her heels came the superb Pied Piper which followed the old aided girdle traverse and free ascents of Mousetrap and Ivy Arete—both technically demanding under-takings at 6b.

Pete Whillance repeated several established climbs and also made an impressive solo of Squirm. Another impressive solo was Derek Jameson's ascent of Hang Out in bare feet!

With the Dunkeld Crags nearing maturity, interest was, once again, directed to Creag Dubh and Glen Lednock. On Bedtimes Barrier Wall, The Ayatollah and The Art of Relaxation epitomize the best face climbing on the former crag. The big, untouched wall right of Oui Oui sported several fine routes, the best of which are Wet Dreams and Acapulco. The latter offers tremendous climbing through roofs on continuously overhanging rock. On Sprawl Wall, Footloose and Fancy Free gives an unforgettable experience whilst Instant Lemon ranks with the very finest on the Eastern Outcrops.

Rumour of a guide sparked off a little interest. An evening visit to Glen Lednock by Spence and Spider McKenzie resulted in two fine strenuous climbs on Eagle Crag. Rab Anderson and Alan Taylor did likewise on Birnam Quarry where they repeated Raspberries, freed Atomic and repeated Spandau Bullet. An impressive performance, bringing the guide well up to date.

1. First Ascent of First Offence, Bedtime Buttress, Creag Dubh.

Photo: Calum Fraser

Creag Dubh

G.R. OS35   673 958

Creag Dubh is the largest and most expansive road-side crag in Central and Southern Scotland, comprising three buttresses, Bedtime, Central Wall and Sprawl Wall, with routes up to 450 feet. It is often best to descend by abseil using one of the many conveniently placed trees at the top of the climbs. The rock is clean and sound, but sometimes the odd loose block may be encountered. Unlike at Craig-a-Barns, the strata lie horizontally which means that the climbing is on flat holds which tend to make the routes strenuous. Generally, most of the climbing is on steep open walls, smooth in appearance and often quite serious. Also, there are a number of large and impressive roofs, most of which are avoided, although some of the more recent climbs take direct lines through them.

At a lower standard there are a number of very enjoyable V. Diffs and Severes.

During a good winter the waterfall forms an impressive free-standing pillar of ice, as yet unclimbed. The line of Oui Oui offers a good III on continuous water ice. However, care should be taken of falling ice.

Access and Accommodation

Leave the A9 road to Inverness at Newtonmore (15 miles south of Aviemore), along the A86 towards Spean Bridge for $3\frac{1}{2}$ miles. There is a lay-by opposite a small gate leading to a large field with two lakes. The crag is clearly visible on the right.

Unfortunately, no natural shelter exists so camping on either side of the road provides the only accommodation. Permission should first be obtained to camp on the lake side. For water, there is a small burn approximately 150 yards west along the road at a left hand bend over a small bridge. The usual amenities are available in Newtonmore and Kingussie.

BEDTIME BUTTRESS

This is the rounded buttress at the far left end of the cliff characterized by a large roof on its upper right hand side.

The crag is split into two sections divided by a vegetated gully/fault. The right hand section consists of a clean continuous wall on which

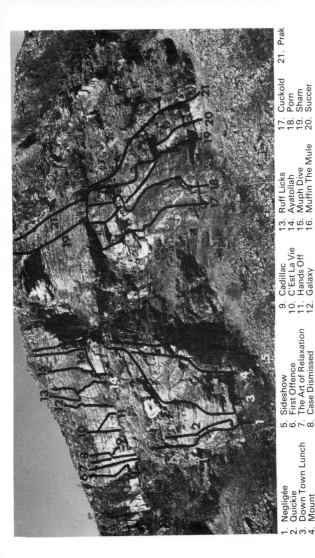

1. Negligée
2. Quickie
3. Down Town Lunch
4. Mount

2. Bedtime Buttress, Creag Dubh.

5. Sideshow
6. First Offence
7. The Art of Relaxation
8. Case Dismissed

9. Cadillac
10. C'Est La Vie
11. Hands Off
12. Galaxy

13. Ruff Licks
14. Ayatollah
15. Muph Dive
16. Muffin The Mule

17. Cuckold
18. Porn
19. Sham
20. Succer

21. Prak

Photo-diagram: Calum Fraser

Cuckold and Porn take lines. The left side features a roof low down with a steep slabby wall above leading to a terrace and the upper tier. This is formed by a long, very steep wall of excellent rock.

Approach: From the bridge in the left hand bend, follow a small path up the stream bed and then cut up the slope to reach the foot of the crag in about 10–15 minutes. The climbs are described from left to right facing the crag.

Descent: Walk left along the top and down a boulder field to reach the foot of the crag. For climbs finishing on the terrace, traverse left and down a short gully beneath and just left of the line of Case Dismissed.

LEFTHAND SECTION

1 **Negligee** 150 ft. Hard Severe*

A good, awkward route. Start at the left end of the roof.

　1.150′. Up short wall to roof, turn this on the left and continue by groove and corner on left to finish.

2 **Quickie** 100 ft. Hard Very Severe 5a*

Sustained and balancy. A useful approach to the upper tier. Start as for Negligee.

　1.100′. After the roof, move right and climb wall going diagonally leftwards to finish up a short crack.

3 **Downtown Lunch** 350 ft. Hard Very Severe 5a, −, 5a*

Two good pitches, technical on the first and thin on the third. Unfortunately, the climb is spoiled by a scrappy middle pitch.

　1.100′. From a raised shelf at the right end of the roof, traverse left by a horizontal crack; surmount bulge and continue rightwards up slabby wall to a belay by blocks.

　2.150′. Ascend to the righthand end of Terrace.

　3.100′. Up side wall on right to gain groove which is climbed with a delicate step left to finish on a slab.

4 **Mount** 250 ft. Very Difficult

Start to the right of Downtown Lunch. A scruffy route.

　Climb the series of short walls and aretes, on the right edge of the buttress to the terrace.

3. First Ascent of Ayatollah, Bedtime Buttress, Creag Dubh.
Photo: Calum Fraser

5 **Sideshow** 100 ft. Very Severe 4c

A loose and serious pitch. Start up and right of Downtown Lunch left of an unclimbed corner crack.

1.100'. Ascend wall diagonally from left to right and climb a loose overhang to finish.

UPPER TIER

6 **First Offence** 85 ft. E3+ 5c**

An obvious feature of this climb is a flake high on the wall left of The Art of Relaxation. Start at a gully/fault slanting to the left.

1.85'. Ascend to a sapling (often wet). Swing out right and ascend wall rightwards to a pocket and protection. Climb leftwards to a flake, up this and move left over bulge to finish.

7 **The Art of Relaxation** 75 ft. E3+ 6a***

Start just left of Case Dismissed. Sustained.

1.75'. Up wall to good break on left, move slightly right and continue up crack line to a ledge and free belay.

8 **Case Dismissed** 75 ft. E3 5c***

A fine bold pitch. Start at the foot of an obvious overhanging crack.

1.75'. Ascend wall and crack to its top. Traverse up and right to a foot ledge before climbing quartz crack above to a block overhang. Move left to a ledge and tree belay.

9 **Cadillac** 50 ft. E3+ 5c*

Start on top of the Crevasse just right of Case Dismissed.

1.50'. Pull on to wall and traverse left to join Case Dismissed at the top of the crack. Continue up quartz crack to ledge and tree belay.

10 **C'est La Vie** 40 ft. E2+ 5c*

Start just right of the crevasse. Poorly protected.

1.40'. Ascend the thin crack to niche. Exit left to finish.

11 **Hands Off** 45 ft. E2 5c*

Start about 15 feet right of C'est La Vie.

1.45'. Gain thin diagonal cracks which lead to the right side of the niche of C'est La Vie. Up wall to finish.

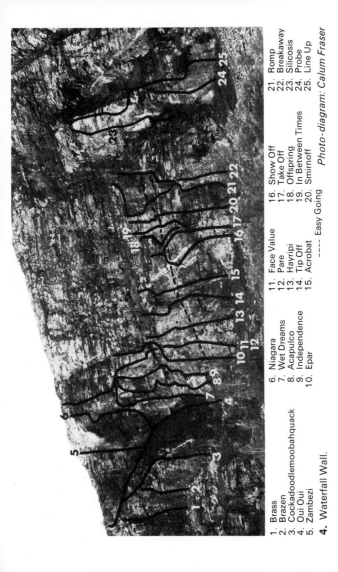

1. Brass
2. Brazen
3. Cockadoodlemoobahquack
4. Oui Oui
5. Zambezi

4. Waterfall Wall.

6. Niagara
7. Wet Dreams
8. Acapulco
9. Independence
10. Epar

11. Face Value
12. Pare
13. Hayripi
14. Tip Off
15. Acrobat

16. Show Off
17. Take Off
18. Offspring
19. In Between Times
20. Smirnoff
---- Easy Going

21. Romp
22. Breakaway
23. Silicosis
24. Probe
25. Line Up

Photo-diagram: Calum Fraser

12   **Galaxy**   80 ft.   E4 – 6a**

Start on wall left of Ruff Licks.

1.80′. Ascend directly up indefinite hairline cracks to a good break. Ascend first left then right up hard wall above to finish at two short finger cracks.

13   **Ruff Licks**   80 ft.   E3 – 5c***

Sustained and pleasing climbing after a bold start. Start at a thin crack which leads to an obvious quartz crack.

1.80′. Ascend to a small tree at two thirds height. Step left and climb crack to the top.

14   **Ayatollah**   80 ft.   E4 – 6a***

A very sustained climb with gradually improving protection. Start as for Muph Dive.

1.80′. Up to roof, step left and pull on to wall above (protection in small quartz pocket). Move left and up to break, continue left and up to another break below small circular quartz recess. Ascend past quartz to gain top break and move left to a junction with Ruff Licks. Move out right and up wall to finish on a slab.

15   **Muph Dive**   80 ft.   E2 5b**

A superb pitch, technical and only adequately protected.

1.80′. Climb the stepped overhanging corner near the right end of the wall.

16   **Muffin the Mule**   80 ft.   E1 5b*

Good, well protected climbing. Start at a thin crack just right of Muph Dive.

1.80′. Ascend awkward crack to a horizontal break; follow this rightwards to a ledge before climbing the slabby wall above.

16a   **Direct Start**   E1 5c*

Gain the ledge by obvious overhanging groove.

RIGHTHAND SECTION
17 **Cuckold**   180 ft.   E1 4c, 5b**

An excellent route with fine contrasting pitches. Start beneath the line of a thin diagonal crack.

1.140′. Gain and climb crack. Where it fades out, make a delicate left traverse into corner; up this to a cramped stance and belay.

2.40′. Up quartz to overhang; turn this on the left and up to ledge and tree belay.

18 **Porn**   180 ft.   Hard Very Severe 5a, 4c**

Good open climbing up the left trending line to the right of Cuckold. Start left of Gham beside a fallen tree.

1.150′. Climb short steep wall and thin crack to gain corner on right. Follow this and left trending line until a right traverse can be made to a small cave belay.

2.30′. Climb thin crack in the steep wall above. Finish up Gham.

19 **Gham**   300 ft.   Very Severe 4c, 4a*

Start beneath a pink quartz jutting shelf near the right end of the crag.

1.70′. Mantleshelf on to ledge and traverse right into corner; climb this avoiding roof on left and continue to a tree belay.

2.100′. Move left on to wall and up to gain crack which is followed to a ledge and tree belay.

3.130′. Up slab and right side of roof to finish.

20 **Prak**   300 ft.   Severe

Climb corner right of Gham, then follow a series of cracks and finally slabs, always to the right of Gham, to finish about 50 feet to the right of Great Roof.

21 **Succer**   200 ft.   E1 5b

Follow the diagonal right-to-left quartz band. Start at an overhanging groove near the right edge of the crag.

1.60′. Up groove and quartz to corner of Gham (loose block and small shrub belay, poor but necessary!).

2.80′. Continue round corner following band of quartz to a belay on Porn.

3.60′. Go left up wall to cracked depression; up this over bulge to finish. Tree belay on left.

LITTLE ROCK

This is the small isolated crag midway between Bedtime and Waterfall Wall, obvious by a two-stepped right-to-left slanting corner with an overhanging wall above. Two routes have been climbed and are on good clean rock.

22   **Hungarian Hamstring**   200 ft   Mild Very Severe 4a, 4c

Good enjoyable climbing.
   1.100'. Up corner crack to ledge and belay.
   2.100'. The continuation to the top.

23   **Un Petit Mort**   50 ft.   E1 5b*

Steep and well protected.
   1.50'. Climb obvious overhanging crack above the first pitch of Hungarian Hamstring.

CENTRAL WALL AREA

The bulk of the climbing on Creag Dubh lies on Central Wall. This comprises three main sections: Waterfall Wall on the left, Great Wall in the Centre and Lower Central Wall tapering down to the right.
   Approach: From the lay-by follow a small path leftwards to reach a fence which leads to the foot of Great Wall in about ten minutes.

WATERFALL WALL

This is characterized by an impressive fall which plunges free for over 100 feet on to the slabs below. The area of rock left of Oui Oui is a steep embankment type wall with a gully trending diagonally left and an impressive area of hanging corners above. Zambezi takes a line up here. The right hand sector consists of a series of steep, open walls and corners tapering away to the tree lined ledge and the corner of Romp.
   Descent: From the top of the crag follow a small path left then down the gully from where Brazen and Brass start.

24   **Brass**   110 ft.   Severe**

This and the next route lie on the embankment wall. A good pitch. Start 20 feet left of Brazen.

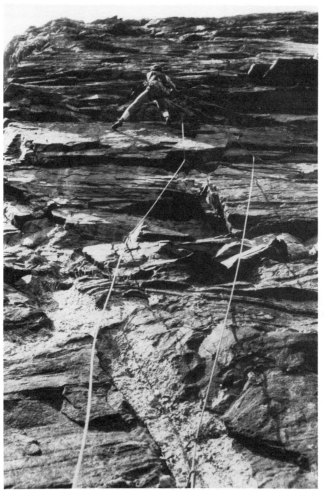

5. First Ascent of Acapulco, Waterfall Wall, Creag Dubh.
Photo: Rab Anderson

1.110′. Traverse right to a ledge and right again to a W shaped roof which is turned on the left to finish up a corner.

25   **Brazen**   120 ft.   Very Severe 5a*

Climbs a steep crack near the right end of the wall. Start low down in the gully at the foot of the crack.

1.120′. Climb the crack to a grass ledge, then trend right up wall above to finish.

26   **Cockadoodlemoobahquack**   200 ft.   Very Difficult

Start to the right of Brazen at the foot of a crack/groove line.

1.100′. Climb crack then traverse up and right to a groove leading back left to a ledge and belay.

2.100′. Finish up easy slabs.

27   **Oui Oui**   300 ft.   Difficult*

Unusual and interesting climbing on clean and sound but invariably wet rock. Climb the corner, pass behind the fall and exit left in two or three pitches.

The following five routes terminates on a grassy terrace with a small bundle of trees. This provides a good abseil descent.

28   **Niagara**   150 ft.   E1 5b**

A tremendous climb with great exposure which follows a line through the slabs and overhangs right of the waterfall. From the foot of the vertical section of the fall, traverse right to a ledge and tree belay.

1.150′. Climb slab and crack on left and follow a steepening groove to a roof. Traverse right and up to a small overhung ledge. Pull into groove to finish over right hand rib.

29   **Wet Dreams**   120 ft.   E2 5b/c***

Climbs the big, open corner bounding the left edge of the wall right of Oui Oui.

1.40′. The first pitch of Acapulco.

2.80′. Up groove to roof, step right and pull into corner. Continue up corner passing a small clump of trees to a ledge and belay. Traverse right under roof to the abseil tree.

30 **Acapulco** 140 ft. E3 + 5b, 5c***

A big bold pitch. Start just to the right of Oui Oui at the foot of a steep left slanting seam of quartz.

1.40′. Climb the quartz seam to a ledge and belay.

2.100′. Move right to groove; up this and step right on to wall; up wall moving left to gain holds over lip of roof. Move right to gain obvious block in overhang, then continue up and right to a good foot ledge. Continue left to finish up a quartz wall.

31 **Independence** 130 ft. E2 + 5b/c***

Start at a shallow groove 20 feet right of Acapulco.

1.130′. Up right-trending grooves to beneath roof and traverse right round rib to a small ledge. Pull through break in overhang (P.R.) and move up and left to a good foot ledge. Ascend wall going rightwards to gain a left trending line. Follow this then near the top move right and up some quartz to finish. Tree belay.

32 **Face Value** 100 ft. E2 + 5c**

Start about 15 feet left of the right end of the roof above the first pitch of Epar.

1.100′. Climb easily to pull over roof and move leftwards to a foot ledge. Continue up the gently overhanging wall on superb holds to a ledge and tree belay.

33 **Epar** 150 ft. Hard Severe*

Start at a small groove beneath the line of an obvious flake crack.

1.40′. Up groove to a ledge and belay beneath the crack.

2.60′. Pull strenuously to reach the flake then continue to a ledge and belay at the right end of the roof.

3.50′. Up groove above to finish.

34 **Pare** 150 ft. Very Severe 4c, 4c

Start at the foot of steep wall between Epar and Hayripi.

1.100′. Up loose groove to enter niche at its top right; up this to grass ledge and spike belay.

2.50′. Up wall behind belay.

35 **Hayripi** 170 ft. Severe**

This climbs the obvious shallow right-facing grassy corner on the right side of the buttress taken by Pare. Sustained and technically interesting.
    1.60′. Climb leftwards ramp and corner to a ledge and belay.
    2.60′. Move right, up ramp and groove to a ledge and belay.
    3.80′. Finish up Epar.

36 **Tip Off** 160 ft. Mild Very Severe 4b*

This enjoyable climb takes an obvious groove up the left side of the overhung recess.
    1.30′. Climb easy corner to ledge and belay.
    2.130′. Up groove above until an obvious step left can be made to gain another groove which leads to the top.

36a *Variation*: **Kneekers Off** Very Severe 4c

Avoid the step left and continue up groove to roof. Exit left to finish.

37 **Acrobat** 150 ft. Hard Very Severe 5a*

Climbs the groove up the right side of the overhung recess.
    1.150′. Up groove to roof (this is gained from directly below), then make a swing right over dubious blocks to the top.

38 **Show Off** 180 ft. Hard Very Severe 4a, 5a**

A committing and strenuous climb with some suspect rock. Start at the left end of a wall leading to the tree-lined ledge.
    1.50′. Up wall to ledge and tree belay.
    2.130′. Pull leftwards on to overhanging wall and follow a line of holds into small groove (P.R.). Up this to gain slab on left. Ascend to roof; step right on to block and finish up groove.

39 **Take Off** 180 ft. Mild Very Severe 4a, 4b*

Climbs the stepped overhanging corner to the right of Show Off. A pleasant route in a good position.
    1.50′. Up wall right of Show Off to ledge and tree belay.
    2.130′. Up left trending corner to a recess on right side of large block. Pull on to this and finish as for Show Off.

40   **Offspring**   140 ft.   Hard Very Severe   5a*

Start to the right of Take Off on the tree lined ledge.

   1.140′. Climb left through break in roof and move up to overhangs right of Take Off. Continue up right wall of corner above, over bulge and exit left to finish.

41   **In Between Times**   120 ft.   E1 5b**

Start midway between Offspring and Smirnoff on the tree lined ledge. Good delicate climbing with scant protection.

   1.120′. Up wall crossing two overlaps at their obvious weak points. Continue up wall and thin crack before traversing left to finish.

42   **Smirnoff**   200 ft.   Hard Very Severe 4c, 5a**

A good technical route which climbs the obvious, tapering, stepped corner. Start beneath some quartz to the right of Show Off.

   1.50′. Up wall and quartz overhang to tree belay.

   2.150′. Bridge up between wall and tree (or climb the wall itself, harder) until possible to pull over roof. Continue up the corner (P.R.) to finish.

43   **Romp**   170 ft.   Very Difficult

Climb the obvious left facing corner in two or three pitches. Much scrambling to finish.

44   **Trampoline**   80 ft.   Very Severe

Start just right of Romp.

   1.80′. Climb the obvious tree-filled corner to ledge and belay.

45   **Breakaway**   200 ft.   Hard Very Severe 4c, 5a**

A varied and interesting climb with a fine second pitch. Start beneath the left hand of two grooves on the steep wall right of Romp.

   1.100′. Climb groove passing large wedged block to a belay on Romp.

   2.100′. Up Romp for a few feet, then follow left slanting quartz crack to roof. Turn this by a bulge on left and continue up slab overlooking the final groove of Smirnoff.

46   **Silicosis**   140 ft   E4 6a, 4c**

This interesting climb follows the obvious and strenuous quartz crack in the wall left of Line Up.

1.60′. Gain obvious niche below and left of crack. Move right and climb crack to ledge with nut belays above.

2.80′. Ascend mossy slab finishing up a short finger crack.

47   **Probe**   80 ft.   Hard Very Severe   5a

1.80′. Climb obvious line just left of the first pitch of Line Up.

48   **Line Up**   480 ft.   Very Severe   4c, 4b, 4a

Pleasant climbing up the left hand of two prominent ribs. Start beneath a crop of ivy.

1.100′. Climb groove to Ivy; step left and up to ledge with nut belays beneath rib above.

2.120′. Ascend rib leftwards to turn overhang on left. Belay below a roof on the right edge.

3.130′. Turn roof on right then climb corner above to tree. Continue to belay below slab.

4.130′. Up slab and scramble to finish.

49   **Route Toot Toot**   500 ft.   Very Severe

A very scrappy route. Start to the right of an overhanging wall on the right hand of two obvious ribs mentioned above.

1.120′. Up mixed rock and vegetation trending left to grassy stance and peg belay.

2.100′. Traverse up left on ledges; go round corner and follow pink quartz fault leftwards until a pull-up rightwards leads to three huge stacked blocks. Go up these to ledges and tree belay.

3.90′. Climb steep corner behind tree to broken ground. Flake belay.

4. Occasional climbing leads to top.

50   **Easy Going**   240 ft.   Hard Very Severe   4c, 4c

A girdle traverse starting from Pare and finishing up Breakaway. Some good climbing.

1.120′. As for Pare, then traverse right across buttress to reach Hayripi. Continue across wall to gain Tip Off at the step left. Descend for a few feet, then traverse right to join Show Off at the short slab beneath roof. Belay.

2.120′. Traverse right to join Take Off; descend this for a few feet until it is possible to traverse wall into corner of Smirnoff. Exit right and cross Breakaway to finish.

GREAT WALL* (See photo-diagram No. 10, pp. 48/49)

The Great Wall consists of two sections. The lefthand section is better defined, being flanked on the left by a vegetated gully capped by a large triangular roof with the obvious lines of King Bee and Nutcracker Chimney to the right. At one third height there is a line of roofs which peters out before the righthand section. Run Free and Erse take fairly direct lines through these roofs above which lies the obvious corner of Brute separating the lefthand section from the right fairly centrally.

On the smooth righthand wall a good reference point is a thin crack leading to a triangular niche. This is Inbred. Bounding the right side of Great Wall is the obvious fault of Rib Direct which separates the Great Wall from the Lower Central Wall.

Descent: The best descent is down the broad, wooded shelf which leads to the foot of Sprawl Wall. Continue down a boulder field and, at a cairn, cut back to the foot of Lower Central Wall.

51 **Men Only** 220 ft. E2 5b, 4c**

Highly spectacular with only adequate protection on the hardest section. Gain a small ledge and belay on the left of a green coloured wall by scrambling up the gully left of King Bee.

1.120′. Traverse right into groove on green wall; up this and overhang to a ledge with small tree. Move right and climb shallow groove to roof; pull over this and traverse left to a ledge and flake belay.

2.100′. Ascend flake and wall to overhang; turn this on the right and continue to a junction with King Bee (P.R.). Step left, climbing corner and overhang to finish.

52 **Run Free** 300 ft. E3 + 4c, 5c, 4c*

Good, devious climbing with a hard, poorly protected second pitch. Start left of King Bee at the foot of an open corner.

1.80′. Up corner and traverse left to a small ledge and belay beneath roof.

2.70′. Traverse right and climb short, steep wall to roof; through this and continue to a stance and belay where Nutcracker Chimney splits.

3.150′. Ascend crack in rib above until a left traverse leads to a black groove. Up groove to small roof; avoid this on right and continue to a ledge and belay. Easy to top.

B

53   **King Bee**   450 ft.   Very Severe 4c, 5a, 4a, 4a**

A classic. Start left of Nutcracker Chimney at foot of obvious arete.

1. 150′. Up rib to tree; move left and up corner to roof. Traverse right through roofs then move back left above lip before continuing up wall to small stance with nut and tree belays.

2. 50′. Move left and up thin crack in bulge. Move left on to exposed edge and pull over small overhang to a P.B. on quartz slab.

3. 100′. Trend rightwards through block overhangs then scramble to terrace with tree belays.

4. 150′. Up corner above to the top.

53a   **Direct Start**   Hard Very Severe 5a*

Where the normal route moves left at the tree, continue straight up through roofs to join the normal route at the belay. A good but poorly protected pitch.

54   **Nutcracker Chimney**   450 ft.   4b, 4a, −

Rather tedious after a good first pitch.

1. 150′. The chimney to a ledge and tree belay.

2. 150′. The continuation right-hand branch to a ledge and belay.

3. 150′. Occasional climbing leads to the top.

55   **Erse**   300 ft.   E2 5b, 4b, 4b**

The first pitch is bold and poorly protected. Start beneath a small groove immediately right of Nutcracker Chimney.

1. 100′. Up grooves and overhang; continue up steep wall to a V notch in the roof. Climb through this and so to a ledge and bolt belays.

2. 120′. Up wall and crack above to a ledge and belay below roof.

3. 80′. Turn roof by bulge on left and continue up corner to a ledge and belay.

N.B. The first pitch can be climbed in two pitches by making right traverse to belay on Brute.

56   **Brute**   350 ft.   Very Severe 4a, 4c, 4a, 4b*

Strenuous but well protected on pitch 2. Start at an open groove to the right of Erse.

1. 80′. Climb groove to a ledge on the right. Continue to a higher ledge and peg belay.

6. First Ascent of Silicosis, Central Wall, Creag Dubh.
Photo: Rab Anderson

2.40′. Traverse right and climb crack in overhang (P.R.) and continue to a ledge and belay at the foot of a corner.

3.80′. Up corner to a ledge and belay on right.

4.150′. Climb slabby wall on left to finish.

57   Jump for Joy   240 ft.   E2 5b, 5b*

Takes a direct line up the wall and two roofs right of Erse. Start as for Brute.

1.120′. Up corner to ledge on right. Move left and up wall to old peg under roof. Pull rightwards over bulge then up and left into groove which leads to ledge and bolt belays.

2.120′. Up easy wall and steepening groove to roof; pull over this, then continue up wall to terrace and tree belays. Descend by abseil.

58   L.M.F.   400 ft.   E1 5a, 5a, 4a*

Takes a direct line between Brute and Erse. Start behind a tree right of Brute.

1.120′. Ascend steep wall to a ledge on Brute. Move left and up to shattered crack (P.R.), follow this and slab to a ledge and bolt belay.

2.130′. Climb obvious quartz groove above to a p.r. Traverse up right to a ledge and belay.

3.150′. The slabby wall on the left as for Brute.

59   Organ Grinder   290 ft.   E1 5a, 5b, 5a*

Start as for The Fuhrer. The route described uses Pitch 1 of the original route and the whole of Organ Grinder variations (not separately described).

1.70′. Up thin crack just left of Fuhrer to gain handrail. Follow this to a niche then climb to ledge and belay on Brute.

2.100′. Climb left of L.M.F. to a roof; traverse right and up wall and slab as for L.M.F. to ledge and bolt belay.

3.120′. Easily up wall to a roof and climb into a groove to the left which leads to a ledge and tree belay.

Descent by abseil recommended.

60   Outspan   200 ft.   E1 5a, 4c*

A steep and poorly protected main pitch up the wall which Organ Grinder avoids on the left. Start as for that route.

1. Men Only
2. Run Free
3. Erse
4. L.M.F.
5. Outspan
6. Over the Hill
7. Migraine
8. Bulger
9. Rib Direct
10. Snoopy
11. Arch Enemy
12. Sweetness
13. Sheath
14. Phellatio
15. Centrespread

Great Wall ... Rising Damp
Lower Central Wall ... Frustrations

Photo-diagram: Calum Fraser

7. Great Wall and L. H. Section of Lower Central Wall.

1.150′. Gain the handrail; follow this for approx. 12 feet, then ascend directly up steep wall on good holds to gain a break (P.R.). Follow this rightwards to a bulge; over this to a large flake then ascend diagonally rightwards as for The Hill to a ledge and belay on that route.

2.50′. Up bulge and slab above as for The Hill.

61   The Führer   150 ft.   E3+ 5c**

A very serious climb, though the climbing is never technically desperate. Start just right of Outspan.

1.150′. Ascend steeply to a good rounded spike. Go leftwards up quartz scoop to gain a plaque-like block. Stand on this, move up and right to a junction with Outspan at the large flake. Ascend slightly leftwards up the fine quartz wall to gain the girdling ledge. Move right a few feet then climb the steep, shallow groove above to ledge and tree belay.

62   The Hill   210 ft.   E2 5b, 5a, 4c***

A magnificent and intimidating climb up the big wall left of Inbred. Start at some rust-coloured rock left of Inbred.

1.60′. Up wall to peg runner (poor). Climb past peg to enter a small groove which is climbed until it is possible to traverse right to a stance and belay in the niche of Inbred.

2.100′. Step up and traverse left to a small niche; continue by slightly descending weakness to gain another niche. Climb wall above to the girdle ledge, then move right to ledge and belay on Inbred.

3.50′. From right end of ledge climb bulge and mossy slab to finish. Belay well back.

63   Over the Hill   120 ft.   E3− 5c***

A superb, very sustained pitch, one of the best on Creag Dubh.

1.120′. After climbing past the peg on the first pitch of the normal route continue up groove and bulge to gain the first niche on the traverse of the second pitch. Move up and right to good spike then ascend diagonally left to gain thin crack. Up this and wall to belay on Inbred.

64   Inbred   350 ft.   Hard Very Severe 5a, 4b, 4a***

A tremendous route. A good introduction to the harder climbs on Creag Dubh. In the smoothest part of Great Wall, an obvious thin crack leads to a triangular niche.

1.80′. Climb crack to peg runner; move left up to triangular niche. Move right up to ledge with bolt belay.

2.120′. Up bulge at left end of ledge and continue up leftward trending line to a tree belay.

3.150′. Climb slabby wall on left to finish.

64a   Direct Finish   100 ft.   Hard Very Severe 5a

Continued from triangular niche of pitch 1 of Inbred.

Belay in the triangular niche. Up thin crack out of niche to join normal route; continue up weakness above going diagonally right to finish up the final crack on Strapadicktaemi.

65   Strapadicktaemi   160 ft.   Hard Very Severe 5a, 5a***

Very enjoyable, varied and well-protected except for a short section on pitch 1. Start as for Inbred.

1.75′. Ascend initial bulge on Inbred, then follow a right slanting crack to a junction with Minge. Up short crack to long narrow ledge; continue over bulge above to a belay on Inbred.

2.85′. Move right to gain leftward slanting crack; follow this to a small overhang; traverse left to gain another crack which leads to the top. Belay well back.

66   Minge   80 ft.   E1 + 5c*

Takes a short hanging groove right of Strapadicktaemi. Start beside Inbred.

1.30′. Traverse right to a ledge and belay.

2.50′. Climb short crack to long narrow ledge (also gained by Strapadicktaemi). Climb the groove (P.R.); exit right and continue rightwards to a stance and belay on Migraine.

67   Migraine   180 ft.   Hard Very Severe 5a, 4a*

Good strenuous climbing up the crack bounding the right side of the Great Wall. Start by a scramble to a ledge and tree belay beneath the crack.

1.100′. Climb the crack over two bulges to a small ledge with numerous nut belays beneath a slab.

2.80′. Follow the left edge of the slabs above to a ledge and belay. Easier to the top.

68 **Bulger**   240 ft.   E2 5b, 5b, 5c*

Sustained and technically interesting. Start from the top of the first pitch of Rib Direct at the foot of a steep rib.

1.80′. Climb crack, move left to a slab, then up overhanging wall on huge holds to a small niche. Ascend wall above past a tiny tree and continue to a ledge and belay on Migraine.

2.80′. Step down and traverse left to the top of the groove on Minge. Bridge across this and continue left on quartz holds to a ledge and belay on Inbred.

3.80′. Pull directly into scoop above and continue rightwards to finish up the final crack on Strapadicktaemi.

69 **Rising Damp**   320 ft.   E1 4c, 5a, 5a***

A magnificent low level left to right girdle of Great Wall. Start as for Run Free.

1.120′. Up corner until possible to traverse right on to the arete of King Bee. Continue right across Nutcracker Chimney and Erse, then follow a line of holds to a belay on the lower ledge of Brute.

2.120′. Step up and traverse right along break (P.R.); continue right and up bulge to large flake. Go right across quartz to a slanting niche and continue to another niche before moving across to a belay in the niche of Inbred.

3.80′. Traverse right and reverse the bulge on Strapadicktaemi to the narrow ledge. Traverse right round corner to join Migraine. Follow this route to a ledge and belay. Finish up Migraine.

70 **Great Wall Girdle**   420 ft.   Hard Very Severe 4c, 4b, 5a, 4a**

A fine natural line. Start as for King Bee.

1.150′. As for King Bee then make a long right traverse to belay at the foot of the Brute corner.

2.120′. Follow break which cuts across the wall to join Inbred; reverse this to ledge and bolt belay.

3.70′. Pull on to narrow ledge and continue right to a stance and belay at the foot of the Migraine Slabs.

4.80′. Finish up Migraine.

LOWER CENTRAL WALL

The lower wall comprises two sections divided by the narrow gully of

--- Frustration
1. Rib Direct
2. Mighty Piston
3. Ticket to Ride
4. Cunnulinctus
5. Phellatio
6. Centrespread
7. Tongue Twister
8. Fiorella
9. Oddli
10. Mirador
11. Scraping the Barrel
12. Goutes d'Eau
13. Gossamer Groove
14. Pshaw
15. Featherlight

8. Lower Central Wall, Creag Dubh.   *Photo-diagram: Calum Fraser*

B*

Fred. The area of rock between Rib Direct and Fred consists of an excellent steep black wall on which Might Piston and Ticket to Ride take lines. Right of this lies the chimney of Cunnulinctus and right again lies another steep wall climbed by Phellatio. This is bounded on the right by a thick growth of ivy. The wall right of Fred, although relatively short, boasts two very good worthwhile climbs.

Descent: Abseil is recommended, although it is possible to scramble to the broad wooded shelf.

71   **Rib Direct**   350 ft.   Very Difficult*

A popular and varied route with an attractive final pitch. Start at a left slanting crack.

1.50′. Up crack to a good ledge and free belay.

2.80′. The obvious groove to a ledge and tree belay under overhang.

3. Turn overhang by crack on left and continue to a ledge and tree belay.

4. Traverse right on to rib which is followed to the top.

72   **Snoopy**   320 ft.   Very Severe 4c, 5a, 4b (1 P.A.)

Start to the right of Rib Direct.

1.120′. Up to a niche and then continue to a ledge with tree belay at the top of pitch 2 of Rib Direct.

2.100′. Step left and climb up to the foot of a mossy slab, up this and move left (1 P.A.) to a belay.

3.80′. Climb up to overhang, using tree, hand traverse right to step on to nose. Continue to the top.

73   **Mighty Piston**   170 ft.   E1 5a, 4c*

The first pitch is sustained and poorly protected. Start right of Snoopy, to the left of a slanting band of quartz.

1.140′. Ascend wall diagonally leftwards; cross a horizontal band of quartz; continue left then up to a ledge and belay.

2.30′. Climb right side of quartz above to finish.

74   **Arch Enemy**   100 ft.   E3 5c**

A fine serious pitch. Start just left of Ticket to Ride.

1.100′. Climb directly up black wall to a point level with the end of an obvious quartz arch. Climb this to its right end, pull up left then continue directly up wall to the top.

9. Ticket to Ride, Lower Central Wall, Creag Dubh.
Photo: Dave Cuthbertson

75   Ticket to Ride   100 ft.   E3 5b***

An excellent and sustained pitch which takes the black streaked wall to the right of Arch Enemy.

1.100'. Ascend rightwards across quartz to a good spike. Continue directly up wall to a small niche. Move left and climb wall to the top. Tree belay.

76   Sweetness   100 ft.   Very Severe 4c

Pleasant climbing up the left bounding rib of Cunnulinctus.

1.100'. Ascend rib direct with a step left at about two thirds height to avoid bulge, then continue to a tree belay.

N.B. This route is only Hard Severe if the chimney is joined at the holly tree. A good variation.

77   Cunnulinctus   220 ft.   Very Severe 4c, 4b**

An enjoyable climb with the hardest moves just off the ground. Start just right of the chimney.

1.100'. Ascend leftwards to join the chimney at a holly tree. Up chimney to a ledge with tree belay.

2.120'. Ascend continuation chimney and move out right to reach a ledge and tree belay.

77a   Sheath Variation   Very Severe 4c*

Instead of making left traverse to holly bush, climb wall directly to join normal route at the belay at the top of pitch one.

78   Phellatio   130 ft.   Very Severe 4c*

A very sustained pitch on good holds. Start at a left slanting groove to the right of Cunnulinctus.

1.130'. Ascend groove and bulge to ledge. Continue up steep wall to ledge and belay.

79   Centrespread   120 ft.   E1 5b*

1.120'. Start as for Phellatio and climb rightward slanting crack to flake. Continue directly up slimy overhanging groove and by wall above ivy crop. Ledge and tree belay on right.

80 **Tongue Twister**   140 ft.   Hard Very Severe 5a*

Devious but good climbing not over-endowed with protection. Start immediately left of the ivy crop.

1.140'. Up groove to roof; pull over this and ascend leftwards to a large block. Traverse back right and ascend to a ledge; continue right to a better ledge and belay.

81 **Fiorella**   120 ft.   Very Severe 4c*

A serious pitch. Start immediately right of the ivy crop.

1.120'. Climb groove and awkward bulge. Continue left then back right to a ledge and tree belay.

82 **Oddli**   100 ft.   Hard Very Severe 4c/5a

Start just left of Mirador.

1.100'. Up wall to scoop. Ascend right then back left to finish directly through some bulges on large flat holds.

83 **Mirador**   120 ft.   Severe

Worthwhile for its two pitches. Start at the foot of a short groove on the left-bounding arete of Fred.

1.60'. Up groove then move right on to arete which leads to a ledge and tree belay.

2.60'. Continue up broken rib to ledge with tree belay. Scramble to the top.

84 **Fred**   300 ft.   Very Difficult

The obvious gully, climbed in three pitches. Exit left near the top.

RIGHTHAND SECTION

85 **Scraping the Barrel**   160 ft.   Very Severe 4c, 4c

Start at the foot of a corner crack on the right wall of Fred.

1.50'. Climb the crack and bulge to a ledge and belay by small tree.

2.110'. Climb the right wall to gain a slab; go up and left before continuing directly over ledges to finish.

86   **Goutes d'Eau**   75 ft.   E1 5a**

Start left of a pine tree on the wall right of the previous route.

1.75'. Climb a shallow groove/crack and bulge to a spike on right. Traverse left across slab to groove on arete; up this to small ledge and belay. Traverse right across slab to tree belay on Featherlight. Descend by abseil.

87   **Featherlight**   75 ft.   Hard Very Severe 5a/b*

Start behind the pine tree.

1.75'. Up wall and overhang then groove to roof. Pull over this then ascend rightwards to a tree belay.

88   **Pshaw**   ·100 ft.   Hard Severe

Steep climbing on doubtful rock. Start to the left of a black overhanging fault to the left of Potato.

1.100'. Climb straight up wall to overhang; turn this on the right by loose corner and climb still looser wall above to finish.

89   **Gossamer**   50 ft.   Hard Very Severe 4c

1.50'. Climb the steep little groove on the buttress between Potato and the black fault.

90   **Potato**   150 ft.   Difficult

1.150'. Climb the stepped rib at the right extremity of the crag.

91   **The Frustration**   280 ft.   E1+ 4c, 5b, 4c*

A left to right girdle of the lower wall. Not as good as Rising Damp, but harder. Start as for Snoopy.

1.80'. As for Snoopy to ledge and belay.

2.70'. From right hand end of ledge step down and traverse right across quartz. Continue above the niche on Ticket to Ride to a belay on Cunnulinctus.

3.130'. Step down and follow quartz band to reach the ledge on Phellatio. Step up and continue across to the ivy crop; ascend wall above then traverse right to finish up Mirador.

SPRAWL WALL

Sprawl Wall comprises three steep buttresses characterized by a very impressive black streaked overhanging wall at its lower right hand end.

Jump So High and Instant Lemon take lines up this. To the left of this face is a long diagonal fault taken by the line of Slanting Groove. To the left of this is an attractive open area of steep grey rock on which Ravens Squawk and Hornet take lines. This area is separated from the end face by a steep mixed wall consisting mainly of vegetation. The end face is obvious by its network of quartz bands capped by a huge roof. The climbs are described from right to left.

The best descent for routes on the right-hand section is by way of a long traverse to the right and a faint path which eventually leads back to the foot of the crag. For routes on the other two walls, follow a small path to the left which leads down to the broad wooded shelf at the top of Central Wall.

92 Slabsville   200 ft.   Mild Very Severe

Not as good as Tree Hee but slightly harder. Start above and right of Tree Hee at the foot of a corner.

1.100′. Up slab on right of corner to a belay under overhang on right.

2.100′. Surmount overhang and climb straight up then right to another large overlap. Surmount this on right then finish up a smooth then dirty slab to terrace.

93 Tree Hee   270 ft.   Severe***

A delightful climb on excellent rock. Start about 50 feet right of the lowest point of the buttress.

1.120′. Make a leftward rising traverse above an overhanging wall, then follow a shallow groove to a ledge and belay on the left edge.

2.150′. Move up and right past holly tree. Ascend slab to overlap; move up left to belay on terrace. Variation possible.

94 Separation   130 ft.   E2 − 5b*

Make an horizontal right traverse to belay at two small trees under the slab of Jump So High. Good climbing.

1.130′. Pull over break in overlap and up to join Jump So High at the end of the traverse. Move right to climb overhanging corner. Exit right and finish up Tree Hee.

95 **Jump so High**   270 ft.   E1 + 4a, 5b, 5a***

Strenuous climbing up the black streaked overhanging wall. Start at the toe of the buttress.

1. Breakaway	4. Line Up	7. Run Free	10. Brute
2. Silicosis	5. Route Toot Toot	8. King Bee	11. L.M.F.
3. Probe	6. Men Only	9. Erse	12. Organ Grinder

10. Great Wall, Creag Dubh.

13. Führer	16. Strapadicktaemi	19. Rib Direct	N. Nutcracker Chimney
14. The Hill	17. Minge	20. Snoopy	× × × × Girdle Traverse
15. Inbred	18. Migraine		- - - - Rising Damp

Photo-diagram: Calum Fraser

1. 100′. Climb deep vegetated corner to a ledge and belay on the right of a slab.

2. 120′. Ascend slab to a small ledge at the foot of an overhanging crack. Climb this to a ledge and belay.

3. 50′. Up thin overhanging crack above; continue trending right to finish.

VARIATIONS
95a   Jump So High Direct   150 ft.   E1+ 5b, 5a**

Start at the foot of a rib to the right of Separation.

1. 80′. Up crack and rib to foot of overhanging crack on normal route. Move right and up wall to belay.

2. 70′. Up crack on right to top.

96   Instant Lemon   150 ft.   E3 5b, 5c***

A superb, serious route which takes a striking line up the overhanging wall left of Jump So High. Start on a flat ledge at the left end of the overhanging wall.

1. 70′. Climb easily up broken quartz flake. Step on to wall and follow hand traverse rail to belay on Jump So High.

2. 80′. Traverse left on huge holds for approx. 15 feet. Move up to a line of small holds which lead leftwards to the base of a groove. Follow this rightwards, finishing up the left side of a corrugated roof.

96a   Direct Start   E4 5c, 5b*

1. 70′. Climb directly up overhanging wall (P.R.) to gain the right hand end of the traverse on the normal route.

2. 80′. From the belay traverse left and climb stepped ramp then ascend rightwards up wall and slab to finish.

97   Stoop So Low   210 ft.   Hard Very Severe 4b, 4c*

A justifiably popular climb with some fine, exposed positions. Start as for Instant Lemon.

1. 130′. Climb a small groove on the left and follow a system of ledges and walls to a shallow scoop below a broken corner. Go up left and climb the corner to a ledge and belay.

1. Instant Lemon
2. Instant Lemon Direct
3. Jump So High Direct
4. Separation
5. Jump So High

11. Sprawl Wall, Creag Dubh.   *Photo-diagram: Calum Fraser*

2.40′. Climb small slab on left; traverse right a few feet and surmount overhang at an obvious break. Continue to a ledge and belay.

3.40′. Climb the walls above to finish.

97a   Direct Finish   60 ft.   Very Severe

Instead of following last pitch, move left and climb the steep, loose wall (P.R.).

98   Slanting Groove   350 ft.   Hard Very Severe 4a, 4b, 4c

The final pitch is steep and exposed. The rock is somewhat suspect. Scramble up right to belay on left of main fault.

1.100′. Climb a ramp and traverse left to a ledge and tree belay.

2.100′. Climb wall behind tree. From the top of a small grassy slope, traverse left across a black wall up to a ledge with tree belays.

3.100′. Gain and climb the obvious groove; pull over an overhang and up short wall to a ledge and belay.

4.50′. Easier rock leads to the top.

99   Ravens Squawk   300 ft.   Severe**

This climbs the obvious left-trending line below and left of Slanting Groove. A grand route in impressive surroundings. Start near the right end of a raised long grass ledge. P.B. recommended.

1.100′. Traverse up to the right following the natural line of the rock, then climb to a steep wall, ledge and belay.

2.150′. Traverse left on to a steep ramp and climb to its apex. Climb through trees and up a short wall to a block belay.

3.50′. Easier to the top.

100   Felix   250 ft.   Hard Very Severe (8–10 P.A.)

A circuitous line between Jack the Lad and Ravens Squawk. The climb probably awaits a second ascent. Start at the foot of a lower wall capped by a large roof.

1.50′. Ascend to roof; traverse left (P.A.) and up to grass ledge and belay.

2.100′. Climb straight up left of Ravens Squawk (P.R.) to gain a stance midway on the traverse ledge of Ravens Squawk.

3.100′. Climb up left to an overhang below a steep slab. Climb this (2 P.A.) and step right to gain cave below large roof. Traverse right and climb through overhang to ledge (aid). Traverse left along ledge and up wall above (2 P.A.).

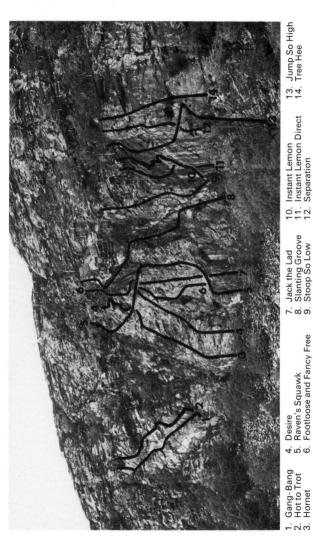

1. Gang-Bang
2. Hot to Trot
3. Hornet

4. Desire
5. Raven's Squawk
6. Footloose and Fancy Free.

7. Jack the Lad
8. Slanting Groove
9. Stoop So Low

10. Instant Lemon
11. Instant Lemon Direct
12. Separation

13. Jump So High
14. Tree Hee

12. Sprawl Wall, Creag Dubh.

Photo diagram: Gary Latter

101   Jack The Lad   210 ft.   E2 5b, 4c, 5b

Start to the left of Felix at a thin crack.

    1.50′. Up crack to ledge and belay.

    2.80′. Up wall to a ledge at about 60 feet. Avoid overhang on right, climb to ledge and belay on Ravens Squawk.

    3.80′. Either finish up Desire or Foot Loose and Fancy Free.

102   Footloose and Fancy Free   180 ft.   E3 − 5c, 5b**

Climbs the open corner to the right of Desire. Start on a long grass ledge just left of Ravens Squawk.

    1.120′. Move left then right into corner (not a smaller black groove just to the left) which is followed to a ledge. Continue up steepening groove. Where it fades out make a rightwards traverse across quartz, then up to ledge and belay on Ravens Squawk.

    2.60′. Traverse right on slab above into corner; move back left and up to overhang. Pull over this and up overhanging wall on large flat holds to an obvious traverse which leads right to a ledge and tree belay.

103   Desire   240 ft.   E2 4c, 5a, 5b**

Good serious climbing with an intimidating final pitch. Start on the right side of the projecting buttress taken by Hornet.

    1.80′. Ascend directly up the right side of the buttress to a ledge and belay.

    2.80′. From the right end of the ledge climb open slabby corner and steepening rock rightwards to a ledge and numerous nut belays on Ravens Squawk.

    3.80′. Traverse up and left to an old peg beneath overlap, move back right and make a long reach to gain a small ledge beneath roof. Turn this on the right then move back left along overhung shelf to finish directly in a very intimidating position.

104   Hornet   350 ft.   Hard Very Severe 5a, 4c*

A strenuous start up the left side of the projecting buttress.

    1.80′. Pull over bulge (loose) to gain and climb a groove which leads to a ledge and belay.

    2.120′. Climb overlap above then climb up and right to a short groove with overhang. Pull over this and continue to a belay on Ravens Squawk.

    3.150′. Finish up Ravens Squawk.

13. First Ascent of Hot to Trot, Sprawl Wall, Creag Dubh.
Photo: Rab Anderson

105 **Gang Bang** 170 ft. Hard Very Severe 5a***

This excellent route follows the obvious left trending groove line in the centre of the quartz patchworked end face. Protection is adequate only.

1.150′. From the lowest point of the crag, move up, right, then back left to a bulge (P.R.). Surmount this and continue to a ledge (possible belay). Ascend left to a roof; pass this direct and continue leftwards to a ledge and belay.

2.20′. Easier rock leads to the top.

105a **Direct Start** Hard Very Severe 5a

Climb the first 30 feet direct to join the normal route at the peg runner.

106 **Hot To Trot** 140 ft. E1 5a, 5b**

Climbs obvious line above and parallel to Gang Bang. Start as for that route.

1.70′. Up to short corner crack; traverse left and ascend groove to small foot ledge beneath quartz block. Step right and up bulge, then continue to ledge and belay under overhang.

2.70′. Pull over roof, then up quartz to another overhang which is avoided on the left. Continue to easy slabs beneath great roof. Traverse left under overhangs and continue left to join Gang Bang at the ledge and belay.

The trees to the right of this belay offer a good means of descent.

Craig Varr

STRATHTUMMEL G.R. OS42 669 590

This group of crags lies half a mile east of Kinloch Rannoch on the north side of the glen only five minutes walk from the road.

Walking uphill one comes to the rightmost lowest crag.

LOWER TIER

1 **Venison** 100 ft.   Very Difficult

1.100′. Climb slab, some grass and a groove at left end of crag.

2 **The Black Hat** 90 ft.   Very Severe

1.90′. Climb short crack on right of grassy central area. Trend left then right below overhangs finishing at a tree.

3 **The Bobble** 70 ft.   Severe

1.70′. After first 30 feet of previous route, trend rightwards up wall passing final overhang by the right.

4 **Dialectic** 125 ft.   Severe

A good route. Start just right of The Black Hat at a rowan tree.

1.125′. Climb on good holds to a flake crack which is followed to the top.

5 **The Great Sod** 90 ft.   Severe

Start below overhang at right end of crag.

1.90′. Go left beneath overhang and up past rowan tree to groove which follows past overhang on right to the top.

Slightly above and to the right of this crag is—

MOTHERS BUTTRESS

6 **Sprog** 100 ft.   Severe

1.100′. Follow left bounding edge of buttress starting from a grassy bay.

7 **The Womb** 110 ft.   Severe

1.110′. Follow obvious crack line into and through a small cave on right hand section of buttress.

8 **Tubes** 150 ft. Severe

1.150′. Follow right hand arete of buttress, traverse left across Womb and finish up behind detached flake.

Some way left and slightly downhill from the top of Mothers Buttress is—

THE UPPER TIER: EAST CRAG
9 **The Black Handle** 90 ft. Very Severe

1.90′. This route takes the ridge between the South and East facets of the crag.

Still further left, easily identified by a large block at its foot is—

THE UPPER TIER: WEST CRAG
10 **Boulevard** 80 ft. Severe

1.80′. The crack and corner just left of the detached block at the crag's foot are climbed.

11 **Curved Slab** 90 ft. Severe

1.90′. Trend left then right from the detached block, up slabs.

12 **Woggle** 90 ft. Severe

1.90′. Takes the obvious crack line 10 feet to the right of the previous route.

Bonskeid Crag

G.R. OS43 908 614

This sadly neglected crag is located behind Bonskeid Farm, approximately 1½ miles along the Tummel Bridge road from its junction with the A9.

Although it does not compare in size or quality with Craig-a-Barns, it is definitely worth a visit, especially for an afternoon on the way north.

The character of the rock is similar to Craig-a-Barns, but rather suspect in places, although this is mainly due to lack of traffic. Most of the climbing is in grooves or on steep walls. Nearly all the climbs have two pitches reaching a maximum height of 160 feet. The south-easterly aspect of the crag enjoys a fair amount of sunshine and dries quickly after rain. Most of these routes have not been checked by the author.

Approach

The best approach to the crag is by a detour to the right from the farm, returning to the foot of the crag in about ten minutes. Permission should be gained to park at the farm.

The crag features a steep wall on its left side. Beneath this lies a short wall leading to a large ledge which runs leftwards on to the Arete, a rather broken V. Diff bounding the left edge of the crag. Towards the right the rock low down is easy angled but above this section lies a very steep series of walls and grooves. The best descent is by a scramble down the right hand side. The climbs are described from left to right.

1 **The Arete**   160 ft.   Very Difficult

Start from the lowest point of the crag and climb the left edge in two pitches.

2 **Johnny Apollo**   160 ft.   Very Severe

Climb the groove line to the left of The Wall, 25 feet right of previous route.

1.110′. Climb corner at right end of short crag to ledge. Ascend groove above, moving left at mid-height and back right below overhang. Step right to large belay ledge.

2.50′. From left end of ledge climb wall as for The Wall.

3 The Wall   160 ft.   Very Severe

Start 15 feet to the right of the previous route at the foot of a rightward slanting groove.

1.100′. Up groove and continue to a recess with a small bush. Go left to a small ledge (P.R.), then climb a rightward groove to a ledge and tree belay.

2.60′. From left end of ledge climb wall above.

4 Lumbar   160 ft.   Very Severe

1.90′. 20 feet to the right of The Wall gain a ledge with a black slab on the right. Climb rightwards up slab, then move up left to a ledge on the wall. Belay below cave.

2.70′. Climb right wall of cave and step left below roof. Finish by steep groove.

5 Diagonal   150 ft.   Very Severe

Start just to the right of Lumbar.

1.150′. Follow obvious rightward trending line to finish up a steep groove.

6 Bonskeid Groove   160 ft.   E1 5b*

The best route on the crag. Start from a small cave 40 feet right of Lumbar.

1.100′. Climb left wall of cave then continue to a ledge and belay below a steep groove.

2.60′. Up groove to the top.

1. The Arête   3. Lumbar   5. Bonskeid Groove
2. The Wall   4. Diagonal

14. Bonskeid Crag.   *Photo-diagram: Calum Fraser*

1. Diagonal   2. Bonskeid Groove

15. Bonskeid Crag.   *Photo-diagram: Calum Fraser*

Craig-a-Barns

Craig-a-Barns is situated on a heavily afforested hillside outside Dunkeld. This is probably the most popular area covered in the guide and justifiably so, taking into account its ease of access, sunny aspect and the sheer quality and variety of its climbs in every category of difficulty. Polney Crag in particular boasts a fine selection of V. Diff—Very Severe graded climbs, while the Cave Crags have routes of higher standard. Unfortunately, Lovers Leap is rather vegetated, although a sense of adventure is well maintained there.

Access and Accommodation

Dunkeld lies about 50 miles north of Edinburgh and 12 miles north of Perth on the old A9 Inverness road, now known as the tourist alternative route through Dunkeld village.

There are several good bivouac spots. A good cave on Polney Crag can accommodate six people and gear quite comfortably. To find this cave: just beyond Myopics follow a forest track, branching from the main road, for about 25 yards. A small path cuts up the wooded slope at this point and leads to the cave. On Cave Crag the flat area around the foot of Rat Race provides adequate shelter in dry weather. On Lower Tier the Lady Charlotte's Cave (rumoured to have been built by a late Duke of Atholl to accommodate one of his paramours) provides good but dark and draughty shelter. There are no official campsites in Dunkeld but there are flat areas at the parking spot for Cave Crags and in the forest under the path beneath Lower Tier. There is no water supply near Polney Crag but plenty of fresh, running water at Cave Crags.

Dunkeld offers the usual services. The tearoom on the south side of the Tay bridge is popular with climbers, likewise the cafe in the main street.

LOVERS LEAP (POLNEY CRAG on p. 66)

G.R. OS52 436 015

Lovers Leap is clearly seen from the road just north of Dunkeld, high on the hill midway between Polney and Cave Crags.

The crag reaches a maximum height of 200 feet and in general the rock is good although heavily vegetated. There are only about half a dozen routes on the crag but there is some potential for those willing to excavate climbs.

16. Tombstone, Cave Crag, Upper Tier. *Photo: Gary Latter collection*

The best approach is as for Cave Crag, then continue following the path sign-posted 'Rocking Stone' and contour round to the foot of the crag. From Cave Crags allow between 15 and 20 minutes.

The best descent is down the righthand side. The first route lies to the left of the main crag.

1   Ash Tree Wall   90 ft.   Very Difficult

Start by scrambling up a wooded terrace to its highest point where the angle of the rock eases quite considerably.

1.90′. Climb between two ash trees then finish up an obvious corner.

2   Tiff Off   170 ft.   Very Severe 4c, 4a, 4c*

Good enjoyable climbing up the rib and groove left of Central Route. Start a few feet left of Central Route at an obvious crack.

1.80′. Climb the crack and step left near a rose bush; continue up groove to a tree belay.

2.30′. Traverse left to a niche, then up to a stance and belay.

3.60′. Surmount overhang above and continue up arete to finish.

3   Central Route   200 ft.   Very Severe 4c, 4a*

A good route, quite sustained and delicate. At the lowest point of the crag there is a 100 foot pillar. Start at a recess at its base.

1.100′. Ascend a few feet then traverse right to a ledge; hand traverse back left at a higher level to a sloping ledge. Continue traversing into a groove with a rose bush. Climb the groove and the grassy ramp above to a ledge and belay.

2.100′. Climb groove in wall above and step left at a steepening in the rock; continue up corner to a ledge and the top.

3a   Variation Start   Very Severe 4c

Climb the layback crack as far as the roof on the right and climb the rib above to join the normal route.

4   Direct Route   200 ft.   Very Severe 4b, 4c*

An interesting route which will improve with traffic. Start at the foot of the obvious corner crack at the lowest point of the crag.

1.70′. Climb crack then move right over vegetation to a tree belay below a roof.

17. Rat Race, Cave Crag, Upper Tier.   *Photo: Gary Latter collection*

C

2.130′. Move right for a foot then climb to a thin ledge; continue for a few feet then traverse left into a groove which is climbed to a steep curving crack. Climb this, step left and continue past a flake to an oak tree. Step left and continue to the top.

5   **Jungle Jim**   180 ft.   Very Severe
Start 50 feet right of corner of Direct Route at pointed rock.
1.70′. Climb wall direct to corner; climb this to a sloping wooded ledge and belay in corner beneath stunted holly bush.
2.110′. Ascend to holly; move right and up groove exiting left on to slabby bay. Continue diagonally rightwards to finish up heathery corner.
Note: This route has not been checked by author.

POLNEY CRAG (See p. 62)

G.R. OS52 435 014

Polney Crag is clearly visible on the right of the road going north. It is split into five sections: Myopics Buttress, Ivy Buttress, Upper Buttress and Main Crag—Left and Right Hand.
Myopics is the isolated overhanging buttress on the far left side. To the right, Ivy Buttress has a series of steep corners and aretes above which are Right and Left Hand cracks and the Upper Buttress. A few yards to the right of Ivy Buttress lies the main crag split by the obvious line of Hairy Gully.

Approach
Follow the old A9 northwards through Dunkeld for about $\frac{1}{2}$ mile until the crag is reached on the right. Park opposite crag on roadside and follow paths to the right hand side of Main Crag—5 minutes.

MYOPICS BUTTRESS

The best descent is to the left.

6   *Myopics Corner*   100 ft.   Very Severe 4c*
Start at the left end of the crag beneath an overhanging groove behind a large tree.
1.100′. Climb awkward groove, step left and climb hidden groove to finish.

18. High Performance, Cave Crag, Upper Tier. *Photo: Rab Anderson*

6a   **Direct Finish**   Hard Very Severe   E2 5c

From the top of the initial groove climb the obvious overhanging crack above. A strenuous pitch.

7   **Coathanger**   80 ft.   A/2

This climbs the weakness up the overhanging wall right of Myopics, entirely on aid.

   1.80′. Peg rightwards to reach main roof, move a few feet left, then up to a roof and rightwards to finish.

UPPER BUTTRESS

Best descent is by a long traverse to the left and down a small gully.

8   **Left Hand Edge**   30 ft.   Hard Very Severe 4c

   1.30′. Climb the left bounding rib of Left Hand Crack.

9   **Left Hand Crack**   30 ft.   E1 + 5c**

A good pitch, steep and sustained.

   1.30′. Climb the corner and rib to finish.

10   **Right Hand Crack**   20 ft.   Mild Very Severe*

   1.20′.   Climb the good jam crack.

11   **Mottled Rib**   100 ft.   Very Difficult*

Not as good as but harder than Hoggs Hindquarters. Start at a steep groove to the left of Hoggs Hindquarters.

   1.40′. Up groove; move left and up to tree belay.

   2.60′. Ascend rib above to the top.

12   **Hoggs Hindquarters**   100 ft.   Very Difficult**

A fine delicate finish after a rather strenuous start above the recess of Duncan Hoggs Hole (apparently the hideout of an old local cattle rustler!).

   1.100′. Climb groove; exit right and move back left on to rib which is followed to the top.

19. Top Pitch, Rat Race, Cave Crag, Upper Tier.
Photo: Calum Fraser collection

13   **The Trap**   30 ft.   Very Severe 5b*

Above and right of Hoggs Hindquarters is a steep little wall.
   1.30′. Climb the awkward cracked wall direct.

IVY BUTTRESS AREA

14   **Psoriasis**   20 ft.   E2 + 6a**

Although short, the landing is unappealing and the hardest moves are at the top. An excellent face climb. Start about 10 feet left of Hot Tips and Ivy Crack.
   1.20′. Ascend wall to a good hold on a small angular niche and make a long reach to finish.

15   **Hot Tips**   50 ft.   E3 + 6b***

Climbs the obvious shallow groove in the left arete of Ivy Crack. A difficult and technically demanding problem.
   1.50′. Pull directly into the groove and climb it to gain a flake crack.

16   **Ivy Crack**   50 ft.   Mild Very Severe 4b*

A well polished classic. Start at the foot of the obvious clean cut corner.
   1.50′. Climb the corner and move left on to rib to finish. Alternatively, harder, climb the continuation of the corner to finish.

17   **Poison Ivy**   50 ft.   Very Severe 5a*

Good jamming after a problematic start.
   1. Up rib right of Ivy Crack to a ledge; step right and up crack.

18   **Poison Arete**   50 ft.   E2 − 5c

Start as for Poison Ivy. Bold.
   1.50′. Gain the ledge and climb direct up arete to finish.

19   **Consolation Corner**   100 ft.   Very Difficult*

A good route. Start just right of Poison Ivy.
   1.50′. Climb short wall formed by huge boulder; move left and up corner to ledge with tree belay.
   2.50′. Finish up two little ribs above.

20. Voie de l'Amie, Cave Crag, Upper Tier.   *Photo: Rab Anderson*

MAIN CRAG—LEFT HAND SECTION

The best descent is to the right, along the top of the crag and down a short gully bounding the right hand side.

20 **Kestrel Crack**   120 ft.   Severe*

A good open climb which follows the line of a slab and bulging flake.

1.80′. Climb shallow crack in slab; traverse right and climb flake to a ledge and belay.

2.40′. The corner above to finish.

20a **Variation Finish**   Very Severe 5a

Climb steep crack in right bounding rib of corner.

21 **Twisted Rib**   150 ft.   Very Difficult**

An interesting and varied route. Start at an obvious rib bounding the right side of the slabs.

1.50′. Up rib to a ledge; move left up to tree, then back right to a second ledge and flake belay.

2.100′. Make a long rightward traverse to some flakes; move left up a slab to a bay, then finish up rib on right.

21a **Direct Finish**   Very Severe 4c*

From the bay climb shallow groove in slabby wall above.

22 **Beech Wall**   120 ft.   Hard Severe**

Steep and technical. Start at a paint mark behind tree to the right of Twisted Rib.

1.120′. Up groove then a second groove to gain the flakes on Twisted Rib. Continue directly to the top.

23 **Pikers Progress Direct Start**   100 ft.   Very Severe 4c.

Start to the right of Beech Wall beneath an obvious flake in the overhanging wall.

1.100′. Gain the flake, pull over this to flakes above and traverse right to finish up Pikers Progress.

21. Warfarin, Pitch Two, Cave Crag, Upper Tier.
Photo: Dave Cuthbertson

c*

24   **The Way Through**   100 ft.   E2 5b*

Technical and quite bold. Start behind a tree to the right of Pikers Direct.
    1.100′. Up wall and overhang; move right and climb a second
overhang; continue to the cracked blocks on the Groove. Finish up this.

25   **The Porker**   100 ft.   E2 5b*

A serious pitch. Start midway between The Way Through and Wriggle.
    1.100′. Good climbing up overhanging wall; move right up slab to
overlap. Pull over this and up left edge of smooth groove to finish.

26   **Pikers Progress**   100 ft.   Mild Very Severe 4c*

To the right of Porker is an obvious break in the overhangs. This and the
next three routes share a start.
    1.100′. Gain the break by traversing from the right; move up right then
leftwards across wall to some cracked blocks. Traverse left round
overhang and follow rib to finish.

27   **The Groove**   100 ft.   Very Severe 4c**

One of the best routes on the crag.
    1.100′. From the cracked blocks on Pikers Progress climb the clean cut
groove to the top.

28   **The Rut**   100 ft.   Very Severe 4c/5a**

A good route with an awkward crux.
    1.100′ Where Pikers Progress starts to traverse left, continue up thin
crack and groove to finish by the last few moves of The Groove.

29   **Wriggle**   100 ft.   Mild Very Severe 4b**

The trade route of the crag.
    1.100′. After the break on Pikers Progress, traverse horizontally right.
Continue by the exposed edge and crack to finish.

30   **Twilight**   100 ft.   Hard Very Severe 5a*

Fine, open climbing. Start at foot of groove on right side of roof with
holly bush just to the right.
    1.100′. Climb groove to holly bush; traverse left into the middle of a
wall which is climbed directly over two bulges to the top.

22. Marjorie Razor Blade, Cave Crag, Upper Tier.

Photo: Rab Anderson

31 **Wriggle Direct**   100 ft.   Hard Very Severe 5a*

Start just right of Twilight.
   1.100′. Up slab to holly bush. Struggle through this and continue up
groove to join normal route.

32 **Scram 79**   90 ft.   E3 5c*

Difficult and serious with suspect rock. Start at the foot of a concave wall
right of Wriggle Direct.
   1.90′. Climb wall left of centre (P.R.) to overhang. Turn this on either
side or climb it direct.

33 **Holly Tree Groove**   100 ft.   Very Difficult*

A pleasant route. Start just right of holly bush.
   1.100′. Climb slanting groove under the concave wall to a ledge. Follow
short chimney to the top.

34 **Recess Route**   100 ft.   Very Difficult*

Start at a rib right of Holly Tree Groove.
   1.100′. Climb left, then back right, to a grassy recess. Finish by a
chimney.

35 **The Creep**   100 ft.   Severe*

Interesting climbing with only adequate protection. Start as for Recess
Route.
   1.100′. Climb rightwards to a sloping ledge; move left over overhang,
then right to a steep nose. Turn this on either side or climb it direct.

36 **Dynamo**   100 ft.   Very Severe 5a*

An eliminate up the wall right of Creep. Good climbing.
   1.100′. Climb shallow groove and overlap direct. Continue to a short
overhanging headwall. Climb this directly to the top.

37 **Nicotine Rush**   120 ft.   E1 + 5b*

A fingery route up the wall parallel to and right of Dynamo.
   1.120′. Climb wall direct to overlap. Pull over this and finish up the
headwall just right of Dynamo.

38   The Excuse   120 ft.   E1 5b*

Good technical climbing with only adequate protection.

1.120′. Up groove right of Nicotine Rush to a small slab beneath overlap. Step right and pull through overlap; continue up slab and flake to the top.

39   Cuticle Creek   100 ft.   Mild Very Severe

Start at a painted C to the left of Cuticle Crack.

1.100′. Climb directly beneath slot in overhang. Climb this and slab to the top.

40   Cuticle Crack   80 ft.   Very Difficult**

A classic in its grade.

1.80′. Climb the obvious crack left of Hairy Gully.

41   Airy Arete   80 ft.   Mild Very Severe 4b

Contrived but enjoyable.

1.80′. Climb the left bounding arete of Hairy Gully.

42   Crescent   80 ft.   Very Difficult

This is the obvious open crack and groove line on the crag above and left of Hairy Gully, just above the finish of Cuticle Crack.

1.80′. Climb vegetated groove to a slab under overhang. Turn this on right and climb groove and crack to exit left.

43   Hairy Gully   80 ft.   Moderate

This is the obvious gully in the centre of the crag. Sometimes used as a descent.

MAIN CRAG—RIGHT HAND SECTION

44   Bollard Buttress   100 ft.   Difficult

1.100′. Climb line of least resistance up the wall bounding the right side of Hairy Gully.

45   Bollard Buttress Direct   100 ft.   Severe*

Slightly harder now that the ash tree has gone. Start at a paint mark right of the normal route.

1.100′. Climb shallow crack and groove line to top.

46   **Springboard Direct**   150 ft.   E1 5b**

The obvious short left-facing groove in the smooth wall right of Bollard Direct. Technical with only adequate protection.

1.150′. Climb wall to break; gain groove above and continue directly to the top.

47   **Live Wire**   120 ft.   E2 6a

Climbs the left arete of Springboard, with runners placed in the initial groove of that route.

1.120′. Climb the arete to junction with Springboard. Go rightwards over overhang to gain and climb arete to the top.

48   **Springboard**   150 ft.   Very Severe 4b**

Good climbing but only adequately protected. Start as for the Direct.

1.150′. Up wall to break; move right and climb brown groove. Step left and up slabby wall to the top.

49   **The Chute**   80 ft.   Very Severe 4c/5a*

This route climbs the slab and quartz bulge right of Springboard. Start from the top of a rock fall.

1.80′. Up slim groove in slab to bulge. Climb crack in bulge and exit either left or right.

50   **Helter Skelter**   80 ft.   E1 5a

Start as for Chute.

1.80′. As for Chute to the quartz bulge. Move left and climb slim groove to finish up the final easy section of Chute.

51   **Pop**   60 ft.   Hard Very Severe 4c*

A sparsely protected little route up the slabby rib right of Chute. Start up from Chute on a small grassy ledge.

1.60′. Gain and stand on a dubious quartz flake. Move up and rightwards to the top.

52   **The End**   150 ft.   Very Severe 4b, 4c***

One of the best routes on Polney Crag. Start right of the rockfall at the foot of a yellow slab.

1.50′. Climb the slab to a bulging nose; climb this to a ledge and belay.

2.100′. Pull over awkward bulge above and continue up slab to a break in the widest part of the overlap. Pull over this and up easy slab to the top.

53   Barefoot—Beginning Connection   180 ft.   E1 5b, 5a**

These pitches constitute one of the best climbs on Polney Crag. Both pitches are quite serious. Start just left of Terminal Buttress.

1.70′. Climb easily to a thin crack; move left and back right to finish just left of Terminal Buttress.

2.110′. Climb the steep, shallow groove (below right) and the slab to an overlap. Pull over this and continue to the top.

54   Terminal Buttress   150 ft.   Hard Severe*

This route follows the obvious corner right of Barefoot.

1.40′. Climb the corner to a ledge and belay.

2.110′. Climb the bulge just left of The End (crux) and gain a recess. Step right, climb crack in overhang and continue up slab to the top.

55   The Duel   100 ft.   E2 5b*

Bold and strenuous, climbing up the overhanging wall to the right of The Beginning. Start from a grass patch behind a tree.

1.40′. Climb to doubtful flake in the middle of the wall. Continue slightly rightwards to good belay in niche.

2.60′. Finish easily up slabs.

56   Carpet Beater   70 ft.   Very Severe 4c*

This short but fine route climbs the obvious left-trending line to the right of an overhung recess.

1.70′. Climb groove then make a left traverse to gain and climb a thin crack to the top. Or, instead of traversing left, climb straight up over bulge on large holds.

57   Spirochaete   90 ft.   Mild Very Severe 4b*

A pleasant layback with good protection. Start at an arrow about 15 feet right of Carpet Beater.

1.90′. Climb layback crack to some grass. Go rightwards up slab to niche then exit left to finish.

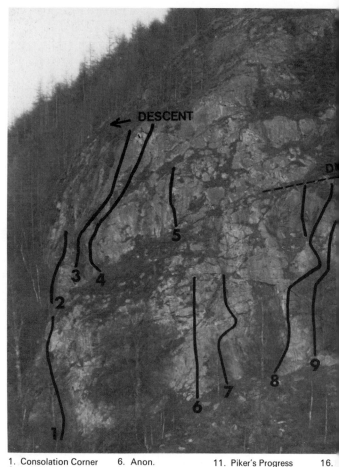

DESCENT

D...

1. Consolation Corner
2. Left-hand Crack
3. Hoggs Hindquarters
4. Mottled Rib
5. The Trap
6. Anon.
7. Kestrel Crack
8. Twisted Rib
9. Beech Wall
10. The Way Through
11. Piker's Progress
12. Rut
13. Wriggle
14. Scram 79
15. Holly Tree Grooves
16.
17.
18.
19.
20.

23. Polney Crag, Craig-a-Barns.

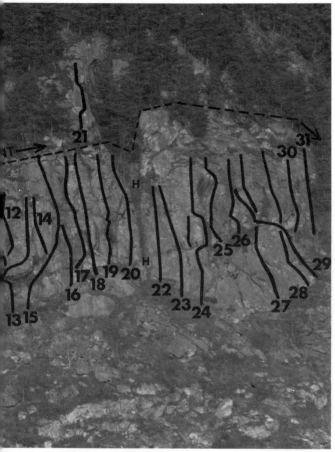

Route	21. Crescent
ep	22. Bollard Buttress
	23. Bollard Buttress Direct
use	24. Springboard
Crack	

25. Chute	29. Terminal Buttress
26. P.O.P.	30. The Duel
27. The End	31. Spirochaete
28. Barefoot/Beginning Connection	H. Hairy Gully

Photo-diagram: Calum Fraser

58 **Girdle Traverse**   600 ft.   Very Severe 4c*

The traverse is described from left to right starting from Kestrel Crack. A long and interesting climb with only two hard pitches. Gain a point beneath the flake on Kestrel Crack and traverse right to the large flakes on Twisted Rib. Belay. Traverse right to the cracked blocks on the Groove. Continue traverse descending into the niche on The Rest. Traverse out of this to join Wriggle (crux). Continue by a long easy traverse descending over outwards sloping slabs to belay on a ledge about 40 feet up Cuticle Crack. Continue across Hairy Gully and the upper slabs of Springboard, then descend to the recess above the quartz crack on Chute. Belay. Continue easily to a belay in the grassy niche on the second pitch of Terminal Buttress. Traverse slab on right to finish.

CAVE CRAG
G.R. OS52 439 018

Viewed from Dunkeld, the Crags appear no more than overgrown and vegetated rocks, but on closer inspection this is not so. Some of Scotland's finest single and two pitch routes are to be found on these crags. The rock in general is completely free of vegetation. It varies from rough and pocketed to smooth and angular in formation. It is of good quality but on some of the more recent routes the odd loose hold may be expected. Most climbs are between 100 feet and 150 feet long and are often split into two pitches.

Approach
Go north through Dunkeld and take the first turning on the right, the A923 to Blairgowrie. Take the second turning on the left up a single track forest road (crossing over a cattle grid); take first left (suitable car park) for $\frac{1}{4}$ mile at which point a small path branches to the right. Follow this, eventually crossing a stream at Lady Charlotte's Cave. After the stream follow the path first left then back right to reach the Lower Tier. For Upper Tier continue up path sign-posted "Rocking Stone", crossing back over the stream and follow a small steep path up the wooded slope to reach the foot of the crag.

Without transport from Dunkeld it is approximately 30 minutes; with transport allow 15 minutes walk.

LOWER TIER
The Lower Tier is split into two distinct sections. The left hand section is obscured by heavy undergrowth but a good reference point is the obvious

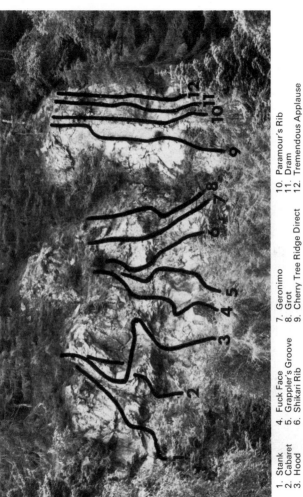

1. Stank
2. Cabaret
3. Hood
4. Fuck Face
5. Grappler's Groove
6. Shikari Rib
7. Geronimo
8. Grot
9. Cherry Tree Ridge Direct
10. Paramour's Rib
11. Dram
12. Tremendous Applause

24. Cave Crag, Lower Tier, Craig-a-Barns.

Photo-diagram: Gary Latter

thin hanging crack of the Civer, with the dirty groove of Stank to its right. Round the corner, across a vegetated gully a more open area of steep rock is found. This is the right hand section. Obvious is the steep corner crack of Cherry Tree Ridge Direct with a steep wall to its right, Dhias and Dram taking lines up this.

The best way off is to continue to the foot of Upper Tier and down the left hand side.

59   The Cludge   120 ft.   Very Severe 4c

Start at a short overhanging corner near the left end of the crag.

1.30′. Climb corner to a ledge and belay.

2.90′. Ascend directly up rib above until a rightward traverse can be made to a thorn tree. Continue right and finish up a rib.

60   In The Shrubbery   120 ft.   E1 5b*

A surprisingly good pitch which climbs the rib to the right of a vegetated corner, not far right of The Cludge.

1.120′. Up vegetated corner. Traverse right on slab under overhang, then climb back left up a ramp. Traverse right to a small birch tree beneath a bulge; pull over this and a second bulge, then continue up rib to finish.

61   Civer   120 ft.   E3 6a/b**

The local test piece. Start at the foot of a thin crack in hanging slab.

1.50′. Up groove to undercling; move up and right to gain hold on arete; continue up crack and flakes to belay.

2.70′. Finish up the second pitch of the Stank.

62   Stank   120 ft.   E1 5a, 5b*

Sustained with two good, contrasting pitches. Start at the foot of a black groove right of Civer. Often wet.

1.50′. Gain the groove from the left on undercuts. Continue for 20 feet then move left and up corner to a ledge and belay.

2.40′. Step right and up groove to a ledge (P.R.). Traverse right to a bulge (P.R.); pull over this to a ledge and flake belay.

3.30′. Trend right to finish.

63   Kaituma   170 ft.   Hard Very Severe 5a, 4c

Start as for Stank.

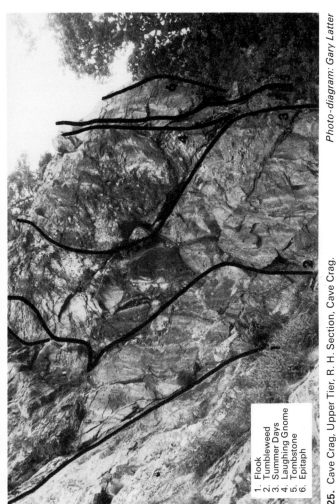

1. Flook
2. Tumbleweed
3. Summer Days
4. Laughing Gnome
5. Tombstone
6. Epitaph

25. Cave Crag, Upper Tier, R. H. Section, Cave Crag.

Photo-diagram: Gary Latter

1.70′. Up Stank for 10 feet. Move right and climb crackline to a ledge on Cabaret. Climb steep wall above going left to a shelf and belay on right.

2.100′. Climb wide crack above; move left and up steep wall to the top.

64   Cabaret   140 ft.   E1 5a, 5c*

Climbs the obvious corner to the right of Stank.

1.70′. Climb the corner over two overhangs to a shelf and belay under roof.

2.70′. Pull on to wall above; traverse right above lip of roof and up to gain Hood. Finish as the crack of Hood Direct.

65   Wot Gorilla   140 ft.   E1 5b/c

A modern eliminate. Start under green overhanging wall just right of Cabaret.

1. Gain ledge above overhanging wall. Pull over roof and then the roof right of Slot. Belay and finish as for Cabaret.

66   The Hood   120 ft.   Hard Severe 4b, 4b***

Sustained and delicate. With only adequate protection, the exposure is strongly felt. Start at a tree stump just right of Wot Gorilla.

1.75′. Ascend until possible to make a long traverse to the right to gain a ramp slab. Follow this turning overhang on right to a roof. Turn this by short wall on right and up to a stance and belay.

2.45′. Step up and traverse left to edge. Climb rib above to the top.

67   Hood Direct   120 ft.   Very Severe 4c, 4c*

Varied climbing with a steep exposed finish. Start round the corner from The Hood beneath an overhang.

1.75′. Climb overhang then traverse left beneath another overhang to join the normal route. Follow this to stance and belay.

1.45′. Climb the obvious overhanging crack above on left.

68   Fuck Face   120 ft.   Very Severe 5a, 4c**

The difficulties are short lived and well protected. Start 20 feet right of Hood Direct.

1.40′. Climb through trees and up overhanging groove to sloping ledge and belay.

2.80′. Pull on to wall above (P.R.). Move right up to recess. Continue rightwards to the top.

1. Lady Charlotte
2. Rat Catcher
3. In Loving Memory
4. Morbidezza
5. Mousetrap
6. Warfarin
7. Rat Race
8. Coffin Corner
9. High Performance

26. Cave Crag, Upper Tier.

Photo-diagram: Calum Fraser

69   **The Stripper**   100 ft.   Hard Very Severe 5b, 5a

An eliminate line left of Grapplers Groove.

1. Climb small groove in arete and continue to join Fuck Face. Move left to block belay on Hood.

2. Climb 10 feet above belay, then traverse steep slab on right to arete. Up this to finish.

70   **Grapplers Groove**   100 ft.   Hard Severe

A poor route which climbs a groove line to the right of The Stripper. Start at arete right of groove.

1.100′. Up arete for 10 feet and move into groove. Up flake overhang. Pass a tree and up groove to ledge. Traverse left above overhang and climb wall to the top.

71   **Shikari Rib**   80 ft.   Hard Very Severe 5a

1.80′. Climb hanging corner and rib between Grapplers Groove and Grot to good ledge beneath overhang. Move slightly right over overhang on small but good holds. Finish by steep but easier ground.

72   **Geronimo**   70 ft.   Hard Very Severe 5b

Worthwhile but poorly protected. Start at top of a grassy ramp 25 feet right of Shikari Rib.

1.70′. Up directly to overhang. Make delicate moves left to reach good holds on overhang. Pull over, step right and climb directly up parallel to Shikari Rib.

74   **Grot**   120 ft.   Severe

Aptly named. Climbs the slab right of Geronimo.

1.120′. Climb slab to a steep wall, traverse left for ten feet, then up to a ledge. Traverse right then finish up vegetation.

RIGHT HAND SECTION
74   **Cherry Tree Ridge**   120 ft.   Difficult

Beyond the vegetated gully lies a well defined ridge. Start at the foot of this.

1.50′. Climb rib to a stance and belay below a steep corner.

2.70′. Turn the corner on the left and continue to the top.

1. Ramp
2. Lilly Langtry
3. Gotterdammerung
4. Voie de l'Amie
5. Hang-out
6. Morbidezza
7. Mousetrap
8. Warfarin
9. Rat Race Direct
10. Rat Race
11. Fall Out
12. Squirm Direct
13. Stand Clear

27. Cave Crag, Upper Tier.   *Photo-diagram: Calum Fraser*

74a **Direct Finish**   50 ft.   Severe*

A fine well protected pitch. Climb the corner to a ledge. Step right and up the edge to finish.

75   **Paramours Rib**   80 ft.   Hard Very Severe 5a*

Bold climbing not over endowed with protection up the right edge of Cherry Tree Ridge.

1.80′. Climb the arete directly to the top.

76   **Dram**   110 ft.   E1 5b*

Immediately right of Paramours Rib is a bulge with a shallow crack in it. A good technical pitch.

1.110′. Climb crack and trend left to the top.

77   **Tremendous Applause**   110 ft.   E1 5b

Climbs the wall 10 feet right of Dram.

1.110′. Climb the wall to reach an obvious cracked groove in the bulging wall. Up this and easier crack above to cross the roof at the V groove.

78   **Dhias**   110 ft.   Hard Very Severe 5a

A steep pitch on large but suspect holds. Start at the end of the buttress beneath a bulging wall.

1.110′. Up wall to a small niche on the left. Continue trending left to Tremendous Applause and right to climb the slabby headwall.

UPPER TIER

The Upper Tier is split into two distinct sections characterized by several obvious grooves. The left end of the crag is bounded by the obvious line of the Ramp. To the right are the groove of Mousetrap and the overhanging crack of Rat Race splitting the very steep central section. This crack leads to a line of roofs which tapers out to the right. The steep central section is bounded to the right by the obvious line of Coffin Corner and the impressive roof of High Performance.

The right hand section shows an obvious slab taken by Flook and a very steep right wall on which Tumbleweed and Summer Days take lines. The obvious groove of Tombstone marks the outer extremity of this section of crag.

The best descent is by a short gully to the left of the crag.

Note: The following three routes lie on the steep flaky wall 200 yards to the left of the Upper Tier.

79 Morningside Warm Up   70 ft.   Very Severe 5a

This takes the obvious left-facing corner in the middle of the wall.

1.70′. Gain the flake crack and climb left over this (crux) into a corner. Climb this and move out right at top to tree belay.

80 Evening Hot Line   75 ft.   Hard Very Severe 5b

Start 7 feet left of Morningside Warm Up where a small tree leans towards the wall.

1.75′. Up wall to ledge (or climb tree to ledge). Go left along ledge to beneath overhang. Climb overhang to finish by steep but easier ground.

81 Hot Line Direct   80 ft.   E2 5b

A difficult climb, loose and poorly protected. Start just right of a large recess at the lowest part of wall.

1.80′. Climb wall on dubious flaky holds to a ledge beneath an overhang. Climb overhang to finish as for Evening Hot Line.

82 Left Edge   120 ft.   Mild Very Severe 4b

An unappealing climb but it makes good use of what rock there is on the sidewall bounding the left end of the crag. Start left of an arete.

1.120′. Climb shallow groove to a crack in a small corner. Up this to a ledge then continue up pleasant rib above.

83 Hos   100 ft.   Hard Very Severe 5a

Start just right of Left Edge.

1.100′. Gain the groove above right; climb this and rib to join the Ramp.

84 Lilly White Lilleth   50 ft.   Very Severe 5b

1.50′. Climb groove in middle of overhanging wall right of Hos.

85 Sidewinder   120 ft.   Severe

Start at a shallow groove to the right of Lilly White Lilleth.

1.120′. Climb up right to a groove. Climb this and turn overhang on

left then step back right and up rib to ledge and belay on The Ramp.
Finish up The Ramp.

86   The Ramp   120 ft.   Hard Severe*

A good route with a steep and bold top pitch.
    1.60′. Up ramp to ledge and belay.
    2.60′. Climb crack above to a ledge. Either step left and climb a sandy
groove or climb steep wall directly above. Both are hard to exit.

The next five routes start from the platform at the top of The Ramp's
first pitch.

87   Lilly Langtry   70 ft.   E2 − 5b*

Steep climbing on good holds. Start at a groove with a small tree.
    1.70′. Climb groove until an obvious step left can be made. Continue
left then move back right to a recess under a bulge. This position can also
be gained by climbing the groove direct-harder. Climb bulge to finish.

88   Gotterdammerung   80 ft.   E3 5c*

Strenuous climbing on suspect rock. Start at a small right slanting groove
to the right of Lilly Langtry.
    1.80′. Up groove to recess beneath block overhang. Ascend this directly
and continue up wall moving left to finish.

89   Voi de l'Amie   100 ft.   E3 + 5c*

The main centre of interest is a short but sensational thin crack
in the headwall above the small ledge on Hang Out. Start as for
Gotterdammerung.
    1.100′. Gain the block overhang. Make an exposed hand traverse to
join the ledge on Hang Out before climbing the thin crack above.

90   Hang Out   120 ft.   E2 5b, 5a*

A good, exposed route which follows the obvious right trending scoop
from the right edge of the platform. Protection is dubious.
    1.60′. Up wall and traverse right into scoop which leads to a small ledge
and belay.
    2.60′. Follow diagonal crack into Rat Catcher which is then followed
to the top.

28. First Free Ascent of Fall Out, Cave Crag, Upper Tier.
Photo: Gary Latter

91 **Pied Piper**   230 ft.   E3+ 5c, 5b***

A fine girdle of the steep central section. The first pitch is hard and committing. A confident second is recommended.

1.130′. Follow horizontal crack to a junction with Rat Catcher (P.R.). Step down and ascend to a pine tree; up this then rightwards to join Morbidezza; reverse the traverse of this into Mousetrap and continue in the same line to a stance and hanging belay on Rat Race.

2.100′. As for Warfarin, pitch 2.

92 **Lady Charlotte**   180 ft.   E5− 6a, 5c***

An audacious route which winds a way up the big wall left of Rat Catcher. Start by climbing the first 15 feet of The Ramp.

1.120′. Climb a small rightward trending groove to a good foot ledge. Ascend left, back right, then left again to better holds on The Pied Piper. Move slightly right and up to gain flake. Follow this and, where it peters out, continue for a few feet before making a left traverse to join Hang Out just beneath the ledge. Belay.

2.60′. Reverse the traverse of Voi de L'Amie, pull over bulge and ascend wall to a small niche. Finish up thin crack.

93 **Rat Catcher**   150 ft.   E3− 5b***

A serious pitch. Start at a small corner to the left of the pine tree. Often wet.

1.150′. Ascend wall and corner to a small ledge (P.R.). Climb right, then back left to join the Pied Piper (P.R.). Continue up groove and exit right to finish.

94 **In Loving Memory**   120 ft.   E5 6b**

Climbs the wall between Rat Catcher and Morbidezza—hard and serious.

1.120′. Up wall behind tree, then the tree itself and traverse right to join Morbidezza at the arete. Step back left and up to peg runner. Climb wall directly to poor holds in small niche (small nut placement in short crack above on left) and continue to a good jug. Move up left to a small right facing corner which leads to the top.

95 **Mousetrap**   130 ft.   E4 6c**

A desperate route in a very intimidating position. Start at the foot of a big groove just right of the pine tree. Often wet.

1.130'. Up corner to bulge barring access to final groove. Climb the bulge (P.R.) and groove above to finish.

96   Morbidezza   120 ft.   E4 6a**

Bold and athletic climbing with gradually improving protection. The route climbs the big overhanging left arete of Mousetrap. Start 10 feet to the right of this.

1.120'. Ascend problematical rib to scoop; move left into Mousetrap; up this for a few feet, then move left to the foot of the arete. Up this arete and left side of large cracked block to finish.

97   Warfarin   180 ft.   E2 5b, 5b**

A tremendous climb, bold and surprisingly delicate. Start beneath short right facing corner to the left of Rat Race.

1.80'. Gain the top of the corner (P.R.) and traverse left into Mousetrap. Ascend Mousetrap for a few feet then traverse back right to a stance and hanging belay on Rat Race.

2.100'. Up slabby wall to corner under roof (P.R.). Continue right traverse to finish.

98   Rat Race   140 ft.   E3+ 5c, 5b***

A magnificent climb with two exhilarating pitches. Strenuous crack climbing on the first with sensational moves over the roof on the second.

1.60'. Climb pod (or its left edge) and crack to a niche at two thirds height. Continue up crack (P.R.) and overhang, then traverse left to a stance and hanging belay.

2.80'. Up slabby wall to corner under roof (P.R.). Traverse 10 feet right and pull through roof on large flange holds. Continue up wall to the top.

98a   Direct Finish   80 ft.   E3 6a*

From the corner under the roof, move out left and pull awkwardly on to the wall above (P.R.) which is climbed to the top.

99   Fall Out   120 ft.   E4+ 6b/c**

A stunning route with a difficult boulder problem start.

Start at a thin crack to the left of Squirm Direct. Ascend crack to recess. Move left and up bulge to pocket (No. 5 rock). Continue immediately right of bolts and make a hard move to join Squirm Direct. Pull boldly leftwards and ascend prow until possible to trend back right to finish up the black groove of Stand Clear.

100   Squirm Direct   120 ft.   E3 − 5c, 5b**

Technical climbing up the groove right of Fall Out.

1.60′. Up groove and transfer into groove on left. Move up to bulge (P.R. poor) and traverse up left to a recess. Continue up right to a ledge and belay on the normal route.

2.60′. Climb the ribbed slab on left (P.R.) to small ledge; move back right and up steep groove with dead tree to finish.

101   Stand Clear   120 ft.   E2 − 5a/b*

A serious climb with poor rock on the final section. Start just right of Squirm Direct.

1.120′. Climb shallow groove and small overhang; cross over Squirm Direct and ascend leftwards into a groove; up groove and move left on to prow which is followed to the top.

102   Squirm   120 ft.   E1 5b, 4b*

A good climb. The crux is short but hard and airy. Start just right of Stand Clear.

1.60′. Up brown scoop and rib to ledge and belay.

2.60′. Traverse left and climb ribbed slab to a small ledge. Continue left on large flakes to the top. Belay well back.

103   <u>Corpse</u>   150 ft.   E1 + 5b**

A fine pitch. A good introduction to the harder climbs. Start just right of Squirm.

1.150′. Climb to right-facing corner. Up this to slab under roof (P.R.). Traverse right and climb awkward crack to the top.

103a   Corpse Left Hand   E1 + 5b

From the slab under the roof, traverse left and up vegetated groove to the top.

104   Coffin Corner   100 ft.   Very Severe 5a***

A splendid climb with some fine, well-protected jamming and bridging.

1.100′. Climb diagonally to enter the corner. Exit right near the top or continue directly to finish.

105 High Performance 100 ft. E3 + 6b***

Bold and gymnastic climbing over the roof right of Coffin Corner. Start from the top of a huge boulder which is gained through a cave.

1.100'. Climb crack in roof to small, overhung ledge. Step right and climb groove (P.R.) to the top.

106 Deaths Head 100 ft. E1 − 5b*

Deceptively steep. Start beside High Performance.

1.100'. Climb cracked groove to bulge; turn this on the right and step back left to finish up a delicate groove. The bulge can be climbed direct— harder.

107 Crutch 90 ft. Severe*

An interesting route with a delicate and exposed final section. Start to the right of the cave entrance at a left-slanting ramp.

1.90'. Up gangway to a ledge. Climb corner above then leftwards across slab to finish up a groove.

108. Marjorie Razor Blade 70 ft. E2 5c, 5a*

A good, well-protected jamming problem. Start immediately right of the cave entrance.

1.50'. Ascend short steep wall to ledge beneath S-shaped crack. Climb this to a ledge and belay.

2.20'. Step left and climb overhanging corner to the top.

109 Noddy 100 ft. Difficult

Climb the vegetated slabs round the corner from Marjorie Razor Blade. A good descent route.

110 Flook 100 ft. Very Difficult*

A pleasant route up the corner between slabs and a steep side wall.

1.100'. Climb the steepening corner until a left traverse can be made to finish up a steep broken wall.

111 Tumbleweed 100 ft. E2 5b*

Steep and fingery with only adequate protection. Start by climbing the first 20 feet of Flook.

1.100'. Pull on to ledge beneath holly bush. Climb overhung gangway

D

on left to a ledge at the foot of a corner. Step right and climb slim groove and wall rightwards to the top. It is also possible to climb the corner above the ledge directly.

112   **Summer Days**   100 ft.   E2 5b*

Steep and spectacular with some interesting moves through the holly bush. Start as for Gnome.

    1.100′. Gain the holly bush by a steep diagonal break which is reached by ascending Gnome. Climb through holly bush (crux) and finish up crack above (P.R.).

113   **Gnome**   80 ft.   Hard Very Severe 5b*

The lower right end of the steep wall forms, in its lower part, a blunt, cracked arete with a very impressive overhanging section above. Start at the foot of this arete.

    1.80′. Climb arete then ascend rightwards to a ledge beneath short open groove. Climb this (P.R.) to the top.

114   **Laughing Gnome**   80 ft.   E4 + 6a**

This climbs the arete continuation of Gnome. Short but very serious.

    1.80′. As for Gnome to the ledge. Step up then traverse left on to the arete which is climbed to gain an easy rib.

115   **Tombstone**   80 ft.   E2 5b**

Good steep jamming and bridging up the obvious groove to the right of Gnome. Start by scrambling rightwards to a ledge and belay.

    1.80′. Follow crack to overhang. Pull over this and continue directly up groove and crack to the top. It is also possible to exit left from the top of the cracked block.

116   **Epitaph**   70 ft.   Hard Very Severe 5a

Start just right of Tombstone.

    1.70′. Climb crack to gain an easy slab which is followed to finish.

Birnam Quarry

G.R. OS52 038 422

The quarry offers the only true slab climbing in the Eastern Crags.

The rock is grey slate and lies at an average angle of 65°. On some of the climbs the surface tends to be a bit flaky but in general it is clean and sound although the frictional qualities leave something to be desired! The quarry is a natural sun-trap and dries very quickly after rain. However, it will seep after prolonged periods of wet weather and during the winter months.

The climbing is of a fairly high standard, thin and serious. Spandau Ballet is an exception—hard but exceptionally well protected.

Access

The quarry is clearly visible from the A9, shortly before the Birnam junction on the north side of the valley. To reach the crag, drive over the bridge into Dunkeld and turn right along the A984 Coupar Angus road for two miles. Limited parking space is available at a gate just beyond Deans Park, a group of white-washed houses. Go through gate and follow track parallel to main road and contour round into the quarry.

The quarry has a big sweep of slab on the right hand side which meets the back wall in a shallow unclimbed corner. To the left of this corner lies the old mine shaft with a partial aid route up the back. On the upper third of the slab the rock tends to be poor.

Descend is by abseil from convenient trees for most of the climbs. The climbs are described from right to left.

1 **Spandau Ballet**   120 ft.   E2 6a**

The first rock at the quarry entrance is a slab split by an obvious thin crack. An excellent climb, very thin but well protected.

1.120′. Climb the crack and depression on its right to a tree belay. The difficulty is inversely proportional to the climber's height!

2 **Counting Out Time**   100 ft.   E3 5c**

A bold and sustained climb which follows the thin crack line up the main slab.

1.100′. Gain the cracks which are followed (delicate) to a short crack. Move up left to overlap; pull over this and gain thin crack which is followed until an obvious right traverse can be made. Tree belay.

3   Slateford Road   80 ft.   E1 5a**

A very good, but poorly protected climb. Start at the foot of a left to right curving overlap.

   1.80'. Up grooves and at an obvious break move left via a scoop to an overlap. Move right to join the last few feet of Counting Out Time. Tree belay.

4   Atomic   100 ft.   E2 5c*

Climbs a shallow corner to the left of Slateford Road. Start as for that route.

   1.100'. From the break left continue to enter a groove. Climb this to an overlap (P.R.) and continue to gain crack which leads to a tree belay.

5   Raspberries   100 ft.   E2+ 5b**

Poorly protected climbing up the slim groove to the left of Atomic. Start beneath the right end of a large block in the overlap above.

   1.100'. Gain the right end of block and traverse left under this (hand placed peg in bore hole above) to move up to a groove which is climbed to a tree on the right.

6   Soft Shoe Shuffle   90 ft.   Hard Very Severe 5a*

Start at a sawn off tree stump below a ramp leading to a cave.

   1.90'. Pull over overlap before Raspberries; move left with difficulty (tied-off channel for protection low right). Follow rightward fault (P.R.) to step into Raspberries just above its crux.

7   Pulse   110 ft.   E2 5b

Climbs the corner left of the Soft Shoe Shuffle peg.

   1.110'. Layback the groove for 80 feet, then traverse right to gain the upper of two belay trees.

8   Desmond Decker   E3 5b/c*

No pitch lengths are available for this and the following route.

   1. Climb the extreme right hand crack of Counting Out Time to belay as for Slateford Road.

   2. Step down from belay to traverse left until a peg is reached. Climb the crack in the wall above. Crux above third peg.

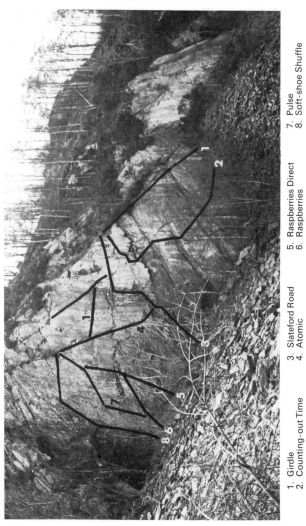

1. Girdle
2. Counting-out Time
3. Slateford Road
4. Atomic
5. Raspberries Direct
6. Raspberries
7. Pulse
8. Soft-shoe Shuffle

Photo-diagram: Calum Fraser

29. Birnam Quarry.

9 **The Fringe**   E4 6a   A Girdle

1. As for Desmond Decker.

2. Traverse left to first peg; step down on to a sloping foothold and make a hard move left to reach a small ledge. Fix No 6 HEX runner. Step up and left to gain Atomic. Belay in tree.

3. Reverse Soft Shoe Shuffle into corner of Pulse.

Abseil off the belay tree.

30. Spandau Ballet, Birnam Quarry.

Farm Crag (Craig Vinean)

G.R. OS52 416 005

This recent discovery has yielded a crop of worthwhile routes. The rock is poorer than on Craig-a-Barns, but its proximity to Dunkeld, attractive outlook and quick-drying qualities certainly recommend it.

The crag faces south east and is situated on the north side of the glen behind Kennacoil Farm about 2½ miles from Dunkeld on the A822 road to Gilmerton and Crieff. To reach the crag turn right over a small bridge and follow a single track road for ⅓ mile. Limited parking space is available at a junction before the farm. Ten minutes walk from the farm to the crag.

The crag has two steep walls, separated by an obvious vegetated gully. The left hand section consists of a steep bulging wall, a ledge system at about two thirds height and an even steeper unclimbed headwall above. The right hand side is defined by more obvious lines bounded to the right by a prominent rib separated from the main crag by a dirty, unclimbed groove. All the routes have one pitch and reach a maximum height of 100 feet. The routes are described from left to right.

Some of these routes may have received earlier ascents than those claimed in this guide.

LEFT HAND CRAG
1   **Chrysalids**   90 ft.   Very Severe 5a*

This route follows a thin crack in the left hand corner of the crag. Good value.

1.90′. Up the crack passing a V-shaped block to a ledge. Pull on to the ramp directly above and continue by the scoop on the left.

2   **Trouble With Lichen**   100 ft.   E1 5a

Aptly named. Start 15 feet to the right of Chrysalids at a faint crack.

1.100′. Follow faint crack directly to a sloping ledge. Up bulge above to another ledge, then climb short wall going slightly left to reach a large tree.

3   **Goliath's Grandad**   100 ft.   Very Difficult

Start 15 feet left of Chrysalids.

1.100′. Follow obvious rising traverse line, crossing Chrysalids below the niche. Continue for 20 feet then move up and left on a broken ledge to reach tree belay.

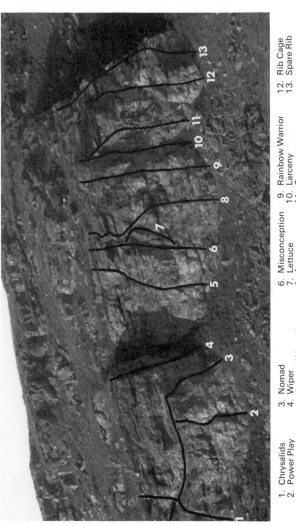

1. Chrysalids
2. Power Play
3. Nomad
4. Wiper
5. General Woundwort

6. Misconception
7. Lettuce
8. Snare

9. Rainbow Warrior
10. Larceny
11. Convergence

12. Rib Cage
13. Spare Rib

Photo-diagram: Calum Fraser collection

31. Farm Crag.

4   Grandads Groove   110 ft.   Hard Very Severe 5b

After a strenuous, fingery start the difficulties ease somewhat. Start 15 feet right of Trouble With Lichen directly below obvious corner.

1.110′. Up right wall of corner to enter upper corner by a short traverse from the left. Climb this to finish.

5   Powerplay   80 ft.   E3 5c**

A steep and strenuous climb with only adequate protection. Care should be taken with a large, loose block near the top. Start at the foot of an obvious crack at the right end of the overhanging section.

1.80′. Up crack (formed by huge block) and step left on to a loose ledge. Pull on to the flange above and layback the arete to gain a hanging loose block. Use this to pull over small roof and up to large ledge below the steep headwall. Finish up Nomad.

6   Nomad   100 ft.   Very Difficult

Start beneath the right end of the large ledge at half height.

1.100′. Climb the broken wall to the ledge then move left to finish up Goliath's Grandad.

7   The Wiper   90 ft.   Hard Severe

Start beneath an open book corner overlooking the vegetated chimney which bisects the crag.

1.90′. Climb wall to small grassy patch. Graze up this to the corner which is followed to finish.

RIGHT HAND CRAG
8   General Woundwort   120 ft.   E2 5b*

Sustained, committing climbing up the hanging groove 20 feet left of Misconception.

1.120′. Gain the hanging groove. At a roof move left for a few feet and back right to a less steep wall. Climb wall to finish up a short corner.

9   Misconception   120 ft.   Very Severe 5a**

A steep and interesting route with some suspect rock. Start at the foot of the obvious central groove.

1.120′. Make some difficult moves to gain the groove proper; up this to a ledge on top of a pillar. Ascend directly above (suspect holds) to a niche, then by crack in roof to finish.

32. Raspberries.   *Photo: Calum Fraser collection*

10   **Lettuce**   120 ft.   Very Severe 4c

Start as for Misconception.
   1.120′. As for Misconception to the foot of the groove. Traverse right to a crack which forms the right side of the pillar. Up crack to top of pillar to finish as for Misconception.

11   **The Snare**   100 ft.   E2 5b*

A good but rather worrying route taking the line of the obvious fork-lightning flake crack to the right of Misconception. Start by scrambling up to a ledge approx. 20 feet right of Misconception or climb crack in wall below to reach ledge.
   1.100′. Up short steep wall to reach flake. Follow this to gain slab above. Move diagonally leftwards across slab to top of the pillar. Pull over the roof rightwards on large flaky holds to a ramp which is followed to the top.

12   **Rainbow Warrior**   110 ft.   E1 5b**

An excellent route which, when seen from a distance, follows an obvious curving ramp rising from the Larceny groove. Start as for Larceny.
   1.110′. Up Larceny for 15 feet, break out of groove by a short steep wall on the left leading to an obvious niche. Continue trending left to the top.

13   **Larceny**   100 ft.   Very Severe 4c*

A good climb which will improve with traffic. Start at the foot of a slabby-looking open groove topped by a holly tree at the end of this section of crag.
   1.100′. Climb the groove and turn a small roof by the left to finish.

14   **Convergence**   100 ft.   Very Severe 4c

Start 10 feet to the right of Larceny.
   1.100′. Climb wall to gain the foot of a very small right-to-left slanting groove. Follow this to small niche below the holly tree on Larceny. Climb roof via thin crack and tree to finish.

15   **Rib Cage**   100 ft.   Very Severe 4c

Start as for Convergence
   1.100′. Trend rightwards up wall to ledge and loose blocks. Move right along ledge almost to the tree-filled groove. A thin, sharply defined

ramp leads through the roof overlooking the groove. Climb this moving left to the top.

16   **Spare Rib**   80 ft.   Severe

A rib bounds the right side of the vegetated groove, giving the line of the route. Start on its right side.

1.80′. Traverse left on to buttress above steep initial wall. Continue up the slabby central section direct, turning bulges at the top on the right.

Glen Lednock

This valley offers a fine selection of good quality climbs in a beautiful setting.

There are two areas of interest to the visiting climber: Balnacoul Castle on the south side of the glen and Eagle Crags on the north.

Although short, Eagle Crags offer a wide variety of steep cracks and walls on excellent rough red granite. A sunny aspect means the rocks dry quickly after rain and are sometimes in condition through the winter. The schist of Balnacoul Castle tends to be very steep and smooth but with some fine crack and groove lines varying between 60 feet and 180 feet in length. The crags are north facing and take some time to dry out. In general, the rock is good but the occasional loose block might still be encountered.

Access and accommodation

Glen Lednock lies northwest of Comrie which is situated on the A85 between Crieff and Lochearnhead. The glen is sign-posted in Comrie at a junction formed by Bonnell and Dundas St. where there is a sharp bend. A single track road is followed for approx. 4 miles at which point Balnacoul is clearly visible on the left with Eagle Crags opposite on the right. The glen road continues for another couple of miles, terminating at a hydro-electric dam.

There are no official camp sites but there is plenty of flat ground and ample water supplies. The usual amenities are available in Comrie.

BOULDERING

The Discodancer area on Central Wall of Eagle Crag offers some good bouldering. On Balnacoul there is a small isolated overhanging wall below and left of Great Buttress with some good strenuous problems, including a route at about H.V.S., 5c in standard.

Balnacoul Castle Crag

G.R. OS52 735 265

There are three main buttresses: Great (north), South and Superlative.

Approach

Leave the road just before a large, white-washed house; follow the dyke and cross the fence by a stile. Cross the river and follow a path first right then back left to reach the foot of Great Buttress in about 15 minutes.

THE GREAT BUTTRESS

This is the rightmost and biggest crag, easily recognizable by a steep crack running its whole length. Bounding the right and left edges of this face are the obvious lines of No Place for a Wendy and The Chancers respectively. The best descent is to follow a small path down to the right. Flanking the Great Buttress on the right is a thin rib.

1   **Spare Rib**   100 ft.   Severe

The start is awkward and there is a spectacular hand traverse at 60 feet!

2   **Piggies Paradise**   130 ft.   E1 + 5b*

A good route, steep and exposed in its final section. Start by scrambling to the groove taken by No Place for a Wendy.

  1.130′. Up groove but follow right hand crack to a ledge with large flake. Continue up flakes moving left into final groove.

3   **No Place for a Wendy**   170 ft.   E2 5a, 5b***

Sustained and strenuous with excellent protection. Start at a groove in the angle where the crag cuts up to the right.

  1.55′. Up groove and step left where it steepens to peg blays in the Great Crack.

  2.115′. Return to groove which is followed to the top.

4   **The Great Crack**   150′.   E2 + 5b, 5c*

  1.70′. Climb corner and crack through overhang and continue until a traverse leads up and right to a belay.

  2.80′. Up crack to the top.

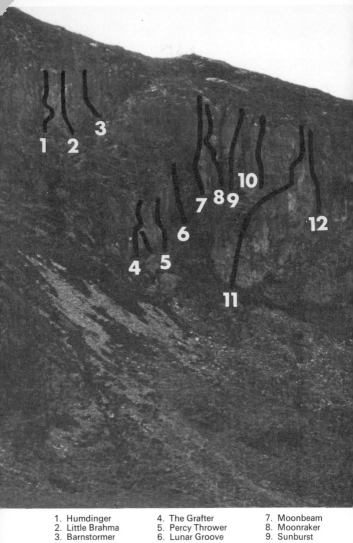

1. Humdinger
2. Little Brahma
3. Barnstormer
4. The Grafter
5. Percy Thrower
6. Lunar Groove
7. Moonbeam
8. Moonraker
9. Sunburst

33. Balnacoul Castle Crag.

10. Tumbledown Wall
11. Carcase Wall
12. Gabrielle

13. Les Alpinistes
14. Chancers
15. Great Crack

16. No Place for a Wendy
17. Piggies Paradise
18. Spare Rib

Photo-diagram: Calum Fraser collection

E

5   The Chancers   150 ft.   E2 + 5c, 5c*

A bold and technical climb. Start at the foot of a corner to the left of Great Crack.

1.100′. Climb corner for 60 feet until level with a gangway on its left. Swing up right to the foot of a steep, thin corner crack. Climb this to a ledge and belay.

2.50′. Climb open corner above to the top of the prow and finish directly by a steep crack.

6   Les Alpinistes Deshabilles   220 ft.   Hard Very Severe 5a

Start as for The Chancers.

1.130′. Follow Chancers to a perched block. Gain the top of the block and follow a ramp leftwards, then go up a short wall to belay in a corner on the left.

2.90′. Climb the corner and follow the leftward trending ramp to belay at a tree.

SOUTH BUTTRESS

This is the next big buttress left of Great Buttress, obvious by the pink coloured Central Groove on its front face. High up to the left of this buttress are two chimneys forming a steep rib in the centre. Sunburst takes this line. The steep chimney on the left is Dividing Chimney with Lunar Buttress forming its southern boundary. The best descent is to gain the top of Great Buttress, then follow path down right side.

In the centre of the cliff a large bracken covered rake rises to a point. To gain the start of the following route, scramble left then right to belay at the foot of a steep corner with a large tree.

7   Gabrielle   85 ft.   E4 6a*

Climbs the right arete of Central Groove. Technical and only adequately protected.

1.85′. Up corner to ledge; step left and up grooves to ledge below Central Groove. Regain groove on right and up to thin diagonal break. Continue up: follow left side of arete and step right to finish.

8   Central Groove   Artificial   A1

Start as for Carcase Wall then traverse behind an enormous flake into obvious open groove. Climb this on aid. The climb appears harder than its A1 rating would suggest.

9   Carcase Wall   270 ft.   Severe

Start at the lowest rocks.

1.80'. Climb a crack to two small trees; transfer to a second crack on the left and go up this to a niche. Continue over grass to tree belay.

2.120'. Move up to base of steep wall and climb strenuously to a flake. Continue trending right to a grass ledge below cracked overhangs.

3.70'. Move right a few feet to reach a slab on right side of overhangs. Traverse delicately round corner on undercuts and up to the top.

9a   Direct Finish   Very Severe 4c

Some loose rock. Start from the top of pitch two. Climb the overhangs above the belay and continue to the top.

LUNAR BUTTRESS

An obvious grassy bay leading to the steep Dividing Chimney marks the boundary between Lunar and South Buttress. The best descent is from the top of North Buttress.

10   Dividing Chimney   70 ft.   Severe

1.70'. Climb the steep left hand chimney.

11   Sunburst   90 ft.   E1 + 5b*

Start a few feet right of Moonraker at the foot of obvious thin crack. Steep but well protected.

1.90'. Climb the crack and its continuation.

12   Moonraker   100 ft.   Very Severe 4c

Start beneath chimney on the right hand wall of the steep buttress.

1.100'. Traverse overhanging wall to arete (P.R.). Up arete then traverse left into Moonbeam. Make a couple of moves up corner, then traverse right into middle of face. Climb direct to large overhang (possible belay). Move left round overhang (P.R.) and up to the top.

13   Moonshadow   130 ft.   E1 5b*

A sustained and strenuous climb up the wall right of Moonbeam. Start as for that route.

1.130′. From the top of the overhanging wall on Moonbeam, traverse right for 15 feet to foot of groove situated on wall overlooking steep chimney. Climb groove to roof; move left round this and up to large roof (possible belay). Traverse left to finish up Moonbeam.

14   Moonbeam   120 ft.   Very Severe 4c**

A good route, steep and well protected. Start beneath an overhang under steep buttress left of chimney.

1.120′. Up short steep wall to ledge. Move right and climb overhanging wall to ledge below groove. Up this to small overhang, move awkwardly left then up wall to finish.

15   The Grafter   70 ft.   Very Severe 4c**

Good climbing, steep and well protected. The route follows a wall and corner crack on the clean area of rock at the bottom left end of the buttress.

1.70′. Up broken rock to ledge below corner crack. Up thin crack to its top, then traverse left until it is possible to go back right to the foot of a corner. Exit from the corner via the crack containing an old tree stump.

16   Lunar Groove   120 ft.   Very Severe 4c

An overgrown and messy climb. Start 20 feet above and right of Percy Thrower at a short corner below a slab.

1.120′. Up corner to slab and gain the foot of a prominent leftward trending groove. Up groove, passing two small trees, to short overhanging crack which leads to a tree. Finish up slab and short wall above.

17   Percy Thrower   60 ft.   Very Difficult

A scrappy route. Start by a rowan tree at the lowest point of the buttress.

1.60′. Climb leftward trending shallow fault to a slab. Finish up wide chimney.

SUPERLATIVE BUTTRESS

This is the long buttress which tapers up and rightwards above Lunar Buttress. The crag is characterized by green rock at its left end, a tree-filled corner in the centre and a cave-like recess towards its right hand end. The climbs are described from left to right. Descend by either side of the crag.

18   **Humdinger**   80 ft.   Hard Very Severe 5a**

Start at the left end of the crag beneath overhanging arete. Exposed and sensational.

1.80′. Climb short wall split by thin crack, then continue up groove to ledge. Traverse left across overhanging wall to arete (P.R.) and hence to the top.

19   **Little Brahma**   80 ft.   Very Severe 4c*

Start to the left of the tree-filled corner.

1.80′. Traverse left on grassy ledge to short groove. Step left on to a slab and wall trending left, then right to the base of rightward sloping crack. Follow crack to finish in niche.

19a   **Direct Finish**   20 ft.   Hard Very Severe 5a

This straightens the climb out. From the base of the crack, climb directly up steep wall to finish by a tree.

20   **Sweat**   60 ft.   Hard Very Severe 4c

Climbs the tree-filled corner.

1.60′. Climb through trees and follow corner crack to the top.

21   **Barnstormer**   70 ft.   Very Severe 4c*

Start on the right side of the buttress at a slab beneath a large roof.

1.70′. Up slab to roof; traverse left up to sloping ledge below short corner. Climb corner, moving left to finish up slab.

1. By the Way
2. Deuxième
3. Premiere
4. Strategies
5. Oddball
6. Get a Grip
7. The Strangler
8. Sultans of Swing
9. The Branch

34. Eagle Crag, Glen Lednock.

10. Cranium Wall
11. Black September
12. Jessicated
13. Tigger
14. Disco Dancer
15. Disco Duck
16. Scarev Monsters
17. Diamond Cutter
18. No Cruise

Photo-diagram: Calum Fraser collection

Eagle Crag

OS52 747 272

The cliff is divided into three main areas interspersed with areas of broken rock. Left hand wall is low down and is long and straggly. Central Wall is the clean wall of rock, well seen from the road to the right of Left Hand Wall. Right Hand Wall is the obvious diagonal cliff.

Approach

Cut directly up to the crag in about ten minutes from the road.

LEFT HAND WALL

This is divided into two main sections by an easy descent rake. The left hand side has an overhanging wall rounding off on to a slab. At the highest point a finger crack cuts up the slab. In the wooded bay left of this a slab leads up to an overhang.

22 **By the Way**   60 ft.   Very Severe 4c

1.60′. Climb the slab and go through the overhang via a large hold to finish up the slab above. Often wet.

23 **Deuxieme**   50 ft.   Mild Very Severe 4b

Start at a rib bounding the left edge of the main wall.
1.50′. Climb the rib stepping right at the top into a corner.

24 **Premiere**   60 ft.   Very Severe 5a*

On the left edge of the overhanging wall is a corner.
1.60′. Climb corner directly until an obvious traverse right leads on to the rib at the foot of the finger crack which is then followed to finish.

25 **Juniors Jinx**   60 ft.   Hard Very Severe 5a**

A good route. Start at the foot of the Premiere corner.
1.60′. Climb cracks in left side of overhanging wall directly to finger crack. Finish up this.

35. First Ascent Black September, Glen Lednock.
Photo: Neil Morrison collection

E *

26 **Strategies**   50 ft.   E1 5b*

Climbs the right arete of the overhanging wall. Start at an easy rake which runs down from the right.

1.50′. Up rake until possible to pull out left on to the arete which is followed. The best finish is to go left into the finger crack.

The right hand section of the cliff is lower and separated by the diagonal rake. The identifying point is the corner recess of the Strangler near the left hand side.

27 **Oddball**   40 ft.   Very Difficult

At the left hand side a series of corners and ledges lead to the rake. Follow these.

28 **Get A Grip**   40 ft.   E1 + 5c**

An excellent hard route. High on the left wall of the recess is a small bow-shaped overlap cut by a vague groove.

1.40′. Climb a wall and groove to a horizontal crack. Take the wall above centrally by the vague groove.

29 **The Strangler**   40 ft.   E1 5c*

1.40′. Climb out of the back of the recess via the crack into an easier groove above.

30 **Sultans of Swing**   40 ft.   Very Severe 4b*

Start in the recess.

1.40′. Follow the diagonal fault right into a niche. Climb the wall above first left then back right.

31 **Sultans Direct**   20 ft.   Hard Very Severe 4c

Start below and right of the niche. Climb cracks to the niche, then follow the original route.

32 **Cranium Wall**   30 ft.   Hard Very Severe 5a*

Start at steep wall at the right end of the wall just before it degenerates into more broken rock.

1.30′. Climb up to an overhang on the right; move right then up to finish.

CENTRAL WALL

This comprises a steep clean wall on the right with a large grass ledge at its top. On the left a wall leads to a ledge above which is another wall guarded by overhangs on its right. In the centre is a corner.

33   Tigger   90 ft.   Mild Very Severe 4b*

Start at the corner.

1.90'. Follow this to the broad ledge, then take a rising traverse left up a slab until an easy groove leads back right.

34   Jessicated   60 ft.   E1 5c*

Left of the previous route are twin cracks.

1.60'. Climb these to the ledge. Above, a break leads up the top wall to easier climbing.

35   Black September   60 ft.   E2 5c**

Slanting half way up the top wall above the ledge is a thin vertical crack. Start directly below this. An excellent route.

1.60'. Climb wall left of Tigger at its highest point to the ledge. Above the ledge a faint crack leads leftwards to a flake. Gain a thin crack; hence to the top.

36   Disco Dancer   60 ft.   E2 6a**

A steep and fingery problem up the right wall broken by a fault. Start in the centre of the wall below a small slot 12 feet up.

1.60'. Up to slot then left to break. Pull up to another break, then go rightwards up the wall above to the grass ledge. Climb a short corner crack above.

37   The Disco Duck   70 ft.   E2 6a**

This route makes a direct start and harder finish to Disco Dancer. Start left of the original start.

1.70'. Climb hard wall directly to break. Follow Disco Dancer but instead of trending right, go straight up to the left edge of the grass ledge. On the left is a break in the overhangs. Go diagonally through this on to easier climbing on Jessicated.

38   **Right Hand Groove**   60 ft.   Very Severe 4c

Start at a wall right of Disco Dancer.
   1.60′. The wall leads to a groove, then the grass ledge. Finish up the corner crack of Disco Dancer.

   Above and right of Central Wall is a clean, apparently slabby wall topped by overhangs.

39   **Scarey Monsters**   70 ft.   Hard Very Severe 5a***

A fine but sustained and poorly protected pitch.
   1.70′. Climb the wall centrally to a ledge below the loose overhangs. Climb out left via a sentry box.

RIGHT HAND WALL

This is the obvious diagonal cliff up and right of Central Wall. Prominent features are the twin diagonal cracks split near their left end by a vertical flake running into a smooth narrow groove above.

40   **Diamond Cutter**   120 ft.   E2 5c**

A fine technical route which climbs the flake and groove.
   1.60′. Climb wall leftwards to a ledge 20 feet up the diagonal crack. Move left and up flakes to hanging belay below groove.
   2.60′. Climb the groove.

41   **No Cruise**   120 ft.   E3 5c**

A steep and strenuous route following the diagonal cracks. Start as for the previous climb.
   1.120′. Climb the wall leftwards to a ledge 20 feet up the crack. Continue up the crack to a cul de sac. Pull out right, then left to finish.

List of First Ascents

CREAG DUBH

Date Unknown	**Rib Direct** B. Halpin, T. Abbey, S. Tondeur	
1959—July	**Nutcracker Chimneys** T. Sullivan, A. Parkin	
Oct	**Brute** T. Sullivan, N. Collingham	
1962—Aug	**Slanting Groove** M. Owen, D. Gregory	
1964—Oct	**Inbred** D. Haston, T. Gooding	
1965—March	**Tip Off** D. Bathgate, I. A. MacEacheran	
Apr	**Tip Off Variation** A. Colvin, A. MacFarlane	
Apr	**King Bee** D. Haston, J. Moriarty, A. Ewing	
Apr	**Tree Hee** H. Small, J. Graham	
May	**Tree Hee Variation** I. A. MacEacheran, J. Knight, R. S. Burnet	
May	**Negligee** I. A. MacEacheran, R. S. Burnet	
May	**Downtown Lunch** F. Harper, A. Ewing, A. McKeith (IPA. FFA Unknown).	
May	**Mount** D. Haston	
May	**Muph Dive** D. Bathgate, R. K. Holt (3 PA. FFA: M. Hamilton, A. Last, 1977—Sept).	
May	**Cuckold** D. Haston, J. Moriarty. (Aid over roof on Pitch 2. FFA P. Boardman, 1974).	
May	**Gham** D. Haston, Miss J. Heron	
May	**Prak** D. Haston	
May	**Epar** D. Haston	
May	**Romp** D. Haston	
May	**Erse** Pitch 1 & 2—D. Haston, J. Moriarty; 3, 4 & 5— D. Haston, Miss J. Heron (aid up to and over roof on Pitch 1. Free var. over roof to right by MacDonald— 1974. FFA by original line by T.)	
May	**Migraine** I. A. MacEacheran, A. McKeith	
May	**Phellatio** A. Ewing, I. A. MacEacheran (direct finish— K. V. Crocket, C. Stead—1972, the way in which the climb is described in this guide).	
May	**Mirador** I. A. MacEacheran, J. Knight, R. S. Burnet	
May	**Fred** A. McKeith, D. Haston, F. Harper, A. Ewing (I. N. Bread, T. Hiebeler climbed under the influence of alcohol)	
May	**Gang Bang** F. Harper, A. McKeith	

1965—May		**Gang Bang—Direct Start** D. Haston, J. Moriarty
	May	**Jump So High** F. Harper, A. McKeith, A. Ewing (5 PA FFA—G. Shields and party—early seventies. Shields also climbed a direct finish. This is now normal finish—FFA: M. Hamilton, K. Spence, 1978).
	June	**Hayripi** D. Haston, M. Galbraith
	June	**Ravens Squawk** M. Harcus, G. Anderson
	Oct	**Show Off** D. Bathgate, J. Renny (Variation start—D. Grey, Miss Thompson, later superceded by ACROBAT).
	Oct	**Take Off** D. Bathgate, J. Renny
	Oct	**Oui Oui** R. S. Burnet, A. McKeith (1st winter ascent: M. Galbraith, E. Woodcock III—January 1966).
	Nov	**Smirnoff** D. Bathgate, J. Brumfit (IPA. FFA Unknown).
	Nov	**Cunnulinctus** R. S. Burnet, A. McKeith
	Nov	**Great Wall Girdle** D. Haston, R. N. Campbell
	Nov	**Fiorella** F. Harper, A. McKeith, J. Knight
	Nov	**Potato** J. Knight, A. McKeith
1966—May 21		**Hungarian Hamstring** A. McKeith, R. Hart, A. Thompson
	Aug	**Cockadoodlemoobahquack** A. McKeith and party
	Aug	**Kneekers Off** J. Brumfit, B. Sproul
1967—May		**Minge** A. McKeith, I. A. MacEacheran, W. Pryde (Aid used. FFA G. Shields and party—early seventies).
	Aug 25	**Slabsville** A. McKeith and party
	Sept	**King Bee Direct** K. Spence, R. Gough
	Sept	**The Hill** K. Spence, J. Porteous
	Sept	**Stoop So Low** K. Spence, J. Porteous
	Sept	**Jump So High Variation** K. Spence, J. Porteous
	Sept	**Trampoline** J. Cunningham
1970—March 10		**Hornet** B. March, G. Cairns
	Apr 11	**Porn** J. Porteous, M. Watson
	Apr 11	**Line Up** I. Fulton, J. R. Houston
	Apr	**Sweetness** B. March, F. Harper
	July 4	**Route Toot Toot** D. Jenkins, C. Stead
	July 11	**Tongue Twister** C. Stead, D. Jenkins
1971—Apr 13		**Outspan** R. Barley, B. Griffiths
	June 27	**Organ Grinder** K. V. Crocket, C. Stead (superceded by Organ Grinder Variations).
	Sept 4	**Mighty Piston** K. V. Crocket, I. Fulton

1971—	Oct 10	**L.M.F.** F. Harper, B. March
	Oct	**Snoopy** B. March, C. Norris (IPA)
1972—	Apr	**Scraping The Barrel** F. Harper, B. March
	Apr	**Brass** A. Fyffe, B. March
	Apr	**Brazen** A. Fyffe, B. March
	Apr	**Pshaw** F. Harper, B. March
	Apr	**Zambesi** G. Shields and party
	Apr	**Niagara** G. Shields and party
	Apr	**Mythical Wall** (Climbs the shallow groove right of the Brute corner above the girdling ledge. Later utilized by the Fuhrer).
	Apr	**Stoop So Low—Direct Finish** B. March, R. Smith
	Apr	**Phelix** B. March, C. Rawlings (8–10 PA).
	Apr	**Sheath** R. G. Ross, H. Henderson, A. Walker
1976—		**Un Petit Mort** R. Baillie, M. B. Smith
	July 23	**Sideshow** D. Cuthbertson, D. Jameson
	July 23	**Run Free** D. Cuthbertson, D. Jameson
	July 24	**Centrespread** D. Cuthbertson, D. Jameson
	Sept 9	**Ticket To Ride** D. Cuthbertson, A. Taylor
	Sept 9	**Men Only** D. Cuthbertson, A. Taylor
	Sept 10	**Strapadictaemi** D. Cuthbertson, R. Anderson
	Oct 27	**Frustrations** D. Cuthbertson, A. Taylor
	Nov 11	**Inbred Direct** D. Cuthbertson, R. Anderson
	Nov 12	**Oddli** R. Anderson, D. Cuthbertson
1977—	Sept 12	**Breakaway** D. Cuthbertson, F. Allison
	Sept 19	**Quickie** D. Cuthbertson, R. Anderson
	Sept 19	**Ruff Licks** D. Cuthbertson, R. Anderson
	Oct 14	**Muffin The Mule** D. Cuthbertson, D. Mullin
	Oct 15	**Rising Damp** D. Cuthbertson, D. Mullin (alt. leads)
1978—	Oct 12	**Case Dismissed** D. Cuthbertson, R. Anderson
	Oct 14	**In Between Times** M. Duff, D. Cuthbertson, Miss J. Small
	Oct 12	**Pare** R. Anderson, A. McAllister
	Oct 13	**Offspring** R. Anderson, M. Duff
	Oct 19	**Easy Going** R. Anderson, A. McAllister
1979—	June 16	**Desire** D. Cuthbertson, I. F. Duckworth
	June 17	**Führer** D. Cuthbertson, I. F. Duckworth
1980—	Sept 29	**Instant Lemon** D. Jameson, D. Cuthbertson (alt. leads).
	Sept 30	**Instant Lemon—Direct Start** D. Cuthbertson, P. Hunter, D. Jameson, C. Lees

1980—Oct 22	**Acrobat** M. Duff, P. Barrass
Oct	**Bulger** D. Cuthbertson, T. Prentice
Oct 23	**Succer** M. Duff, P. Barrass
Nov	**Over The Hill** D. Cuthbertson, R. Kerr
1981—	**First Offence** D. Cuthbertson, C. Fraser
	Independence D. Cuthbertson, R. Kerr, C. Fraser
	Ayatollah D. Cuthbertson, R. Kerr, C. Fraser
	C'Est la Vie M. Lawrence (solo)
	Galaxy D. Cuthbertson, M. Lawrence
	Separation M. Lawrence, D. Cuthbertson
	Hands Off M. Lawrence, D. Lawrence
	The Art of Relaxation D. Cuthbertson, R. Williamson
	Footloose and Fancy Free D. Cuthbertson, R. Williamson
	Organ Grinder Variation D. Cuthbertson, R. Williamson
June 6	**Arch Enemy** D. Cuthbertson, R. Anderson
June 6	**Probe** D. Cuthbertson, R. Anderson
June 7	**Silicosis** D. Cuthbertson, R. Anderson
June	**Jack The Lad** D. Cuthbertson, R. Anderson
June	**Goutes d'Eau** D. Cuthbertson, R. Anderson
June	**Featherlight** D. Cuthbertson, R. Anderson
June	**Gossamer** R. Anderson, D. Cuthbertson
June	**Cadillac** D. Cuthbertson, R. Anderson
June	**Acapulco** D. Cuthbertson, R. Anderson
June	**Hot To Trot** D. Cuthbertson, R. Anderson
June	**Wet Dream** D. Cuthbertson, R. Anderson (possibly climbed earlier with aid).
Aug.	**Jump for Joy** D. Cuthbertson, R. Duncan, A. Taylor

CRAIG-a-BARNS

1959–1960—	**Myopics Corner** I. G. Rowe
	Left Hand Crack N. McNiven (aid FFA I. F. Duckworth and party—1976).
	Right Hand Crack N. McNiven
	Hoggs Hindquarters R. N. Campbell
	The Trap N. McNiven
	Ivy Crack P. Brian
	Poison Ivy R. N. Campbell
	Consolation Corner P. Brian

1959–1960—   **Kestrel Crack** R. N. Campbell (variation finish—R. N. Campbell).

Twisted Rib R. N. Campbell (Direct Finish—P. Brian).

Beech Wall R. N. Campbell

Pikers Progress R. N. Campbell (Pikers Var. later superceded by Twilight).

The Groove R. Smith

The Rut N. McNiven

Wriggle R. N. Campbell

Holly Tree Groove R. N. Campbell

Recess Route J. Proom

The Creep R. N. Campbell

Cuticle Crack P. Brian

Crescent R. N. Campbell

Hairy Gully Unknown

Bollard Buttress R. N. Campbell

Bollard Buttress—Direct P. Brian

Springboard—Direct D. Bathgate (2 PA FFA D. Jameson—1978).

Springboard R. N. Campbell

The Chute R. N. Campbell

The End R. N. Campbell

Terminal Buttress R. N. Campbell

Girdle of Polney R. N. Campbell

Ash Tree Wall I. G. Rowe

Central Route I. G. Rowe

Direct Route R. A. Hockey (alt. start R. A. Hockey).

Cludge R. N. Campbell

Civer I. G. Rowe (first pitch A2. FFA Murray Hamilton —1977).

The Stank G. and R. Farquhar (2 PA on pitch 2. FFA M. Coustan—1974).

Hood R. N. Campbell

Hood—Direct Start B. Robertson

Hood—Direct Finish N. MacNiven

Fuck Face D. Haston

Grot R. N. Campbell

Cherry Tree Ridge R. N. Campbell

Cherry Tree Ridge—Direct R. A. Hockey

Girdle of Lower Cave Crag R. N. Campbell

1959–1960—	**Left Edge** R. N. Campbell
	The Ramp P. Smith
	Mousetrap I. G. Rowe (A2/A3 aid reduced to 4 PA for aid by G. Smith. FFA D. Cuthbertson—1979).
	Squirm—Direct D. Bathgate (A3 5 PA FFA M. Hamilton, A. Taylor—1976).
	Squirm N. MacNiven (1 PA FFA M. Hamilton, A. Taylor—1976).
	Corpse N. MacNiven (A2/3 PA FFA M. Hamilton, A. Taylor—1976).
	Coffin Corner P. Smith
	Coffin Arete G. and R. Farquhar (A2/5 PA FFA D. Cuthbertson, renamed High Performance 1978).
	Crutch A. Wightman
	Noddy P. Smith
	Flook R. N. Campbell
	Gnome B. Robertson (anonymously, a direct finish was later added with 1 PA FFA M. Couston—1974).
1963—	**Rat Race** R. N. Campbell, J. MacLean (Pitch 1 FFA M. Hamilton. Pitch 2 climbed to roof from where new direct finish taken 1 PA—1976. Original 2nd pitch climbed free by D. Jameson and party FA of Warfarin. First on sight completely FA M. Graham—1978).
1965—	**Airy Arete** A. McKeith
	Hairlip R. N. Campbell (later superceded by Cabaret).
1966—Apr	**Cuticle Creek** I. G. Rowe, P. MacDonald
May	**Rat Race—Direct** I. G. Rowe, D. S. B. Wright (FFA D. Cuthbertson, K. Johnstone—1980).
1967—June 3	**Coathanger** J. R. Dempster, K. J. Martin (an aid route A3).
July	**The Way Through** K. Spence, R. Sharp
1969—	**Pikers—Direct** I. G. Rowe
	Squirm—Direct Finish J. Porteous
	Ratcatcher A. Petit, K. J. Martin (A3 almost entirely aid. FFA D. Cuthbertson, M. Hamilton—1976).
	Ivy Arete (FFA D. Cuthbertson, R. Anderson—1980). Renamed Hot Tips
Oct 4	**Green Cheese** K. J. Martin (climbed entirely on aid. A3. FFA D. Cuthbertson, M. Lawrence—1981). Renamed In Loving Memory

1969—Dec 8	**Spirochaete** J. Camerson, C. Norris
	Fall Out M. Forbes, G. Miller (FFA D. Cuthbertson, G. Latter—a two-day effort, 1982)
1971—March 13	**Carpet Beater** C. Norris, A. Moore
1972—	**Hang Out** M. Forbes, G. Miller (4–5 PA FFA M. Hamilton, D. Cuthbertson, D. Jameson)
1974—	**Sidewinder** D. Brown, R. Anderson, D. Cuthbertson
1976—June	**The Beginning** D. Cuthbertson, M. Hamilton (top roped previously by D. Cuthbertson).
June	**Tumbleweed** D. Jameson, D. Cuthbertson
Oct 3	**Paramours Rib** B. Clarke, G. Rooney
Oct	**Deaths Head** D. Cuthbertson, A. Taylor, M. Hamilton
1977—March	**Marjorie Razor Blade** D. Cuthbertson, M. Hamilton
July 3	**Jungle Jim** R. Baker, A. McCord
1978—Sept 5	**Warfarin** D. Jameson, G. Nicol, M. Duff
Oct 10	**Tombstone** D. Cuthbertson, M. Duff
Oct 21	**Pop** M. Duff, A. Kelso
Nov	**Stand Clear** M. Duff, R. Anderson, G. Clarke
Nov	**Epitaph** P. Hunter, C. Lees
Nov 21	**Lilly Langtry** M. Duff, R. Anderson
Nov 26	**Kaituma** A. Taylor, R. Anderson, M. Duff
Nov	**Summer Days** D. Cuthbertson, R. Anderson
Nov	**Wriggle—Direct** D. Cuthbertson, R. Anderson (possibly climbed before).
Dec 12	**The Stripper** M. Duff, R. Anderson
1979—March 11	**Morningside Warm Up** P. Hunter, C. Lees
Apr 22	**Tremendous Applause** M. Duff, R. Anderson
Apr 23	**Dhias** M. Duff, R. Anderson
May 6	**Shikari Rib** P. Hunter, S. Drummond
May 6	**Geronimo** P. Hunter, S. Drummond
May 21	**Evening Hot Line** P. Hunter, S. Drummond
May 21	**Hot Line—Direct** P. Hunter, S. Drummond
June 16	**Cabaret** R. Anderson, R. Bruce, M. Duff
June 24	**Morbidezza** D. Cuthbertson
Aug 23	**Scram 79** P. Hunter, C. Lees
Sept 5	**Gotterdammerung** P. Hunter, R. Williamson (previous top rope inspection).
Sept	**Voi De l'Amie** D. Cuthbertson, R. Anderson, M. Duff
Sept	**In The Shrubbery** D. Cuthbertson, R. Anderson
Sept	**The Porker** M. Hamilton, K. Spence

1979—Sept	**Psoriasis** A. Taylor (solo)
1980—Apr	**Lady Charlotte** D. Cuthbertson, M. Duff (pitch 2 added April—D. Cuthbertson, K. Johnstone).
Apr 24	**Pied Piper** D. Cuthbertson, M. Duff
May	**Mottled Rib** D. Cuthbertson, Miss G. Saxon
June	**Dynamo** R. Anderson, D. Cuthbertson
June	**The Excuse** D. Cuthbertson, R. Anderson
Aug	**The Duel** P. Hunter, C. Lees
Aug	**Barefoot** D. Cuthbertson, P. Hunter
Sept	**The Laughing Gnome** D. Cuthbertson, D. McCallum
Sept	**Wot Gorilla** N. Morrison, T. Hay
Sept	**Hos** D. McCallum, R. Williamson
Sept	**Live Wire** M. Duff, P. Barrass
Oct	**Helter Skelter** A. Taylor, R. Anderson, K. Spence
Nov	**Poison Arete** D. Cuthbertson, T. Prentice, I. Duckworth
Nov	**Left Hand Edge** D. Cuthbertson
Nov	**Nicotine Rush** R. Kerr, D. Cuthbertson
Nov	**Twilight** D. Cuthbertson, R. Kerr

GLEN LEDNOCK

1973—Oct 10	**Moonbeam** I. Conway, T. Connelly
Oct 17	**Percy Thrower** D. Baker, T. Connelly
1974—March 31	**Grafter** D. Baker, I. Conway
March 31	**Moonshadow** I. Conway, D. Baker
Apr 3	**Humdinger** I. Conway, D. Baker
Apr 6	**Barnstormer** I. Conway, D. Baker
Apr 7	**Little Brahma** I. Conway, D. Baker (Direct finish added by N. Morrison).
Apr 10	**Moonraker** I. Conway, T. Connelly
May 15	**The Great Crack** I. Conway and party (some aid. FFA E. Grindley, I. Duckworth—1975).
June 12	**Lunar Groove** I. Conway, D. Baker
June	**Sweat** I. Conway
June	**Dividing Chimney** J. Porteous, R. MacDonald
June	**The Chancers** E. Grindley, Miss E. Brookes
June	**No Place for a Wendy** M. Hamilton
1979—	**Premiere** R. Stewart, B. Hogg, N. Morrison
	Strategies I. Duckworth, B. Duncan, N. Morrison
	Get a Grip I. Duckworth, B. Duncan, N. Morrison

1979—   **The Strangler** I. Duckworth, B. Duncan, N. Morrison
                     Sultans of Swing R. Stewart, B. Hogg, N. Morrison
                     Sultans—Direct C. Calow, B. Hogg
                     By The Way I. Duckworth, C. Calow
                     Deuxieme I. Duckworth (solo)
                     Tigger N. Morrison, B. Hogg
                     Black September N. Morrison
                     Right Hand Groove Anon.
                     Oddball Anon.
                     Piggies Paradise D. Cuthbertson, I. Duckworth,
                     N. Morrison
                     Gabrielle D. Cuthbertson
1980—   **Cranium Wall** I. Duckworth, C. Calow
                     Jessicated I. Duckworth
                     Disco Dancer I. Duckworth
                     Disco Duck N. Morrison
                     Scarey Monsters N. Morrison, B. Hogg
1981—June   **Diamond Cutter** K. Spence, J. MacKenzie
                     No Cruise J. Mackenzie, K. Spence

BIRNAM QUARRY
1979—Sept 27   **Counting Out Time** M. Duff, J. Handren
      Sept 11   **Slateford Road** M. Duff, G. Clarke (top roped
                     previously).
1980—   **Atomic** M. Duff, A. Russel, B. Stitt (1 PA FFA
                     D. McCallum—1981).
      Aug 31   **Raspberries** M. Duff, A. Russel
1981—May   **Spandau Ballet** D. McCallum, J. Handren, R. Anderson
      June 7   **Soft Shoe Shuffle** D. McCallum, J. Handren
      July   **Pulse** M. Duff, D. McCallum, C. Barlow

FARM CRAG
1978—June 12   **Misconception** Stickland, Owen, Dowds
      June 20   **Goliath's Grandad** Strickland, Owen
      June 20   **Larceny** Owen, Stickland
      Aug 13   **Grandads Groove** Cheesman, Owen (alt. leads.
                     A harder start and finish later added by M. Duff,
                     G. Hornby).
      Aug 13   **Convergence** Owen, Cheesman

1980—Oct 12   **Rainbow Warrior** M. Duff, G. Hornby
         Oct 13   **Chrysalids** M. Duff, G. Hornby
         Oct 13   **Trouble With Lichen** G. Hornby, M. Duff
         Oct 13   **Nomad** G. Hornby
         Oct 13   **Snare** M. Duff, G. Hornby
         Oct 15   **Wiper** G. Hornby, M. Duff
         Oct 15   **Rib Cage** M. Duff, G. Hornby
         Oct 15   **Spare Rib** G. Hornby
         Oct 15   **Power Play** M. Duff, G. Hornby
         Oct 26   **General Woundwort** M. Duff, R. Anderson
         Oct 26   **Lettuce** M. Duff, R. Anderson

Index of Climbs